FREE SPEECH

OR

PROPAGANDA?

Other Books by Marlin Maddoux

America Betrayed
The Selling of Gorbachev

FREE SPEECH

OR

PROPAGANDA?

How the Media Distorts the Truth

MARLIN MADDOUX

THOMAS NELSON PUBLISHERS
Nashville

To our sons,
Mark, David, and Tim,
and to our daughter,
Marla

Contents

PART ONE

THE NEWSPEAK BATTLE FOR AMERICA

A Really Big Show in the Barnum and Bailey Tradition

A hysterical girl knelt over a young man lying on the grass. With arms outstretched, she pleaded for someone to help him. But there was nothing anyone could do. The young man was dead. It was May 1970.

After a long hard day at work, I felt good settling down to an evening with my family. Finally I could relax, unwind. While Mary put the finishing touches on dinner, I slipped into my easy chair. It welcomed me as an old friend. I picked up the newspaper, glancing only momentarily at the black-and-white television in the corner of the den. The evening news was just beginning.

I had read just a few lines on the front page when something on the television screen caused me to look up. But all I saw was rioting college students railing at the government, burning their draft cards, taunting police officers, and raising their fists in defiance of everything in general. I'd seen it all before. Who needed a rerun of these spoiled brats giving yet another collective obscene gesture to all things American? I yawned and almost turned back to my paper.

But this time was different. Something dreadful had happened. I put my paper down and watched the unfolding drama.

Periodically, we had been seeing crazies blowing themselves up with homemade bombs they had put together to terrorize the nation, but so far we hadn't seen the kind of killing and bloodshed that usually accompanied this type of unrest. Not until now.

As the news anchor reported the happenings at Kent State University that May evening, I watched the ensuing pandemonium. The rioting, it seemed, had gotten out of hand and some national guardsmen, fearful for their own lives, had opened fire on the unruly mob. According to the newscaster, people had been killed. Before it was over, two women and two men were dead, and eight others were wounded.

At that moment, America lost her innocence. In a few years, something had happened to our nation's soul. It was simply brought to a head at Kent State.

When the newscast ended, I flipped the television set off and sat in my chair staring at the darkened screen. It seemed unbelievable, even though I had feared for a long time that it would come to this. I didn't know where America was going after that day.

For months I had feared that the television networks' unremitting drumbeat of coverage of every riot and rebellion—whether of twenty people or of twenty thousand—was propelling us to just such a moment. Night after night I had seen the radicals who were calling for the destruction of America being paraded as heroes across my television screen. They were given a national platform from which to spout forth their venom and disdain of our country and its institutions. And all the while they were calling on us, the American people, to burn down our society and to build some kind of New-Age utopia on its ashes.

These revolutionaries knew exactly what the networks wanted, and they gave it to them. They let the network assignment editors know where the next riot would be, and they staged it early enough to get pictures on the six o'clock news.

For weeks after viewing the events at Kent State, a gnawing feeling right in the pit of my stomach told me that something was wrong in the way the news media had played up these revolutionaries. They hadn't shown us both sides. By the sheer hours of coverage they gave to each little radical group, they were planting in the viewers' minds the idea that these were the true Americans and that we should all join them.

What I had been seeing was a giant Barnum and Bailey circus. In a way that old P. T. Barnum would have loved, the networks marketed "news and information" in snake-oil fashion. And in the process, they helped the radicals destroy America. What was most horrifying was that nobody seemed to care.

Although I watched the evening news for years and years, I never saw the other side presented. The television screen was dominated by the left. Anyone who dared stand up to the revolutionaries was never given national publicity. These people were not the heroes. That distinction was reserved for the Huey Newtons, the Abbie Hoffmans, the Jane Fondas, the Timothy Learys. Heroism was afforded organizations such as Students for a Democratic Society, the Black Panthers, the Simbianese Liberation Army, and a hundred other nondescript, ragtag, college-campus groups of so-called intellectuals.

To be honest, I don't think the majority of the college students across America who took part in the rioting, the flag burning and general destruction, took it seriously at first. It was just a giant "beer bust," a nationwide party, a night out to howl. For some it was a chance to get on national television, to be seen marching in a protest led by some denim-clad, bewhiskered sociology professor. For many young people, it was simply the thing to do. They were away from home, away from the restraints of their parents. They could scream out their obscenities and voice their adolescent rebellion without worrying about being sent to their rooms without supper or having their allowances cut off.

And all the while the musicians and rock stars were busy writing music to extol the use of drugs and promote Eastern mysticism and call for worldwide revolution. They said it was "blowing in the wind." It was the "dawning of the Age of Aquarius."

Many students were caught up in what they thought was nothing more than a good time. But the events at Kent State changed all that. Suddenly it wasn't fun anymore.

But the hard-core, doctrinaire revolutionaries were delighted to see it happen. They had studied Lenin and Mao Tse Tung and Castro and Che Guevara, and they knew what they needed to fuel their revolution—the blood of martyrs. The standard Marxist tactic—which most of them learned from a Marxist college professor—was to create so much civil unrest that the country would become ungovernable, then push the police forces until they reacted with violence. They could then call on the "people" to avenge the blood of those who died in the struggle to bring "freedom to the masses." They were convinced that when this happened the entire nation would rise up in arms against the "oppressors"—whoever they were.

But it didn't happen. Rather than rebellion and civil war spreading like an uncontrollable forest fire, the American people—especially the young people—began to have second thoughts. Things began to cool down. The rioting, destruction, and rebellion were losing their glamor. Reason began to return. The revolutionaries were no longer the patriots. The rioting was not the Second American Revolution. People began to see just how ugly the movement was.

For several years prior to this, people had called me on my radio talk show in Dallas, Texas, and expressed their view that we had biased media here in America. I usually shouted at them, "Bring me facts; then I'll take your argument seriously!" I would leave the radio station and say to myself, *What a bunch of phonies. Can't they think of anything better to talk about than so-called bias in the media? After all, this country was made great through freedom of the press. We even have an amendment guaranteeing it. These people have been reading too much John Birch Society stuff.*

After carrying on this little conversation with myself, I'd feel better. I trusted the media. Why shouldn't I? Then I'd wonder, *Is it possible they could be right? No way! But then again, to be fair and in the interest of good journalism, maybe I at least should have a look at their viewpoint.*

Now the Kent State tragedy backed me into an intellectual corner and forced me to take a long, hard, critical look at my own assumptions about the news media and how they choose to present events, people, and ideas to the American public.

I started to analyze the news, not just let it pass unfiltered into my brain. What unfolded before my eyes both amazed and frightened me.

A consistent pattern began to develop. In fact, there wasn't a nickel's worth of difference among the "Big Three"—ABC, CBS, and NBC. The stories were basically the same; the bias in their coverage was the same. It became frighteningly clear that the television screen was dominated by the radical left. And opposing views were virtually closed out.

Even after the Kent State tragedy, the media's favorable coverage of the radicals continued unabated. Everyone was blamed for the tragedy except the screaming mobs. Anyone who dared stand up to these media revolutionaries was given minimal coverage. And that was given grudgingly.

During those turbulent years, I found I was growing more and more concerned about our country's direction. Unless something was done, we were headed straight for disaster. Whatever I was doing—whether working or driving or reading—I couldn't shake the feeling that America was being conned, and conned on a grand scale. Worse yet, the media were part of the problem. They actually seemed to be reveling in the destruction of our society. And nobody was challenging them!

The first person I remember making an attempt to call the media to task was Vice President Spiro Agnew. When he was later forced out of office in disgrace, it became even more difficult for anyone to speak out and demand account-ability from those who were responsible for reporting the news. The word *McCarthyite* was slapped on anyone out of step with the liberal cavalcade.

While traveling across the nation in those days, I often tuned in to some of the hundreds of talk shows on radio. Many cities were then developing what has come to be called an "all talk" format. These stations had bull pens full of talk show hosts who conducted wall-to-wall talk pro-grams.

Whether it was St. Louis, New York, Chicago, Los Angeles, or Dallas, talk show stations, I noticed, all seemed to adhere to the same formula. Their hosts also seemed to fit into a very definite profile. Let me introduce you to the talk show hosts who filled the airways all across America.

THE MESSIANIC PSYCHOLOGIST

First of all, every station had what I call the *Messianic Psychologist*. This was generally a woman who had all the answers to everybody's problems. Usually a dyed-in-the-wool "secular humanist," she would countenance no men-tion of biblical morality. If a caller dared make any reference to restraint in the pursuit of sexual pleasure and "fulfill-ment," the "psychologist's" shocked reaction seemed to exclaim: "Where did *you* come from? Don't you know the world has changed? We've outgrown those antiquated ideas!"

The "psychologists" assumed the role of Apostles of

the New Morality, quickly spreading the "good news" that sexual freedom had finally arrived. When it came to pursuing sexual pleasures, women could now be as aggressive as men. The pill, they claimed, had announced the beginning of the party, and no one had better dare stand in the way. "We're playing by new rules now," they told us.

What a difference a decade makes. After a few years of such juvenile indulgence, the party atmosphere suddenly began to fade. We were discovering that this so-called sexual freedom came with a horribly high price tag: disillusionment, heartbreak, loneliness, not to mention venereal diseases, herpes, and the biggest partybuster of them all—AIDS.

Yet the radio psychologists refused to veer from their old line: "Never be 'judgmental' about anything." If someone did happen to have regrets, maybe even emotional problems, the radio psychologists had the answer for them as well: "Go get therapy."

Psychologists and psychiatrists were touted as the priests and ministers of secular humanism, the new religion of humanity. They promised to solve all our problems by helping us rid ourselves of the real culprit—religion. Religion in general, they said, and Christianity in particular. Why? Because Christianity teaches about sin. And, don't you know, *nothing* is sin anymore. In this day and age it's just "different strokes for different folks." And those good ole radio psychologists were going to help us get rid of our religious "hang-ups" so that we, too, could swing into the party and enjoy ourselves.

THE HARVARD GURU

The second type of talk show host was what I call the *Harvard Guru.* These were the people who were going to help listeners develop their "inner selves" or their "latent abilities" or their own "psychic abilities." These guys literally gushed with Eastern mysticism. Why, they had all "been to the mountain," don't you know? They had sat at the feet of the great masters—all in Psychology 101 at one of the big state colleges with professors who had forgotten all about the subjects they were hired to teach.

What was happening was that taxpayers' money was being used to pay instructors to seduce these young people—along with hundreds more gullible, naive students—into everything from transcendental meditation to astral projection.

Although none of these *Harvard Gurus* had actually made it to India yet, that was the dream of each and every one of them. Until that time, they were dedicated to bringing "the light" to their listening audiences. We were entering the "Age of Aquarius," we were told. The gurus proceeded to prove it by telling us all the planets had lined up single file and were spewing out goodness and light or some such nonsense.

Naturally these gurus were pacifists who felt all the soldiers of the world should stick flowers in the barrels of their guns, sit down together with the enemy, "smoke a joint," and work things out. They thought Gandhi was the greatest and considered the music of the Beatles to be the hymns of the New Age. They believed in Jesus—that He had slipped away to India during the "missing years," that is, and had received His wisdom at the feet of the Indian gurus. They were certain we could all become little "Christs" if we just followed His lead. They told us that joy, fulfillment, happiness, and world peace would all come to pass if only the whole world would sit cross-legged, palms up, and say "om" long enough. And you know what? Their audiences believed it all.

Harvard Gurus chose their words carefully. They avoided occult terms. Any suggestion of possible occultism or satanism was strictly out of bounds. Theirs was nothing more, we were informed, than an exercise in "human potential," and everyone was encouraged to experiment. Thousands of gullible people called in to radio shows across the country to get a "reading" about some important area of their lives. The psychics, of course, were all too willing to oblige.

THE JERK

The usual talk show format simply wouldn't work without the third standard host, the one I call *The Jerk*. Everywhere I went, I heard the likes of him. The only difference I noticed from region to region was his accent. Certainly his ravings were the same. So much so, in fact, that I often suspected they had all been hatched out of test tubes in the broadcast laboratories of Obnoxious U.

The Jerk was the guy who had all the answers—to everything. He had gone to college and had learned the following irrefutable facts: Christianity is on its way out. America is the major cause of all the world's ills. Capitalism is exploiting the world's resources and keeping the Third-World nations steeped in poverty. Conservatives, those throwbacks to the Dark Ages, are clinging to a political system in its death throes. Christians are people who have developed mentally not too very far beyond the Neanderthal stage; it's the liberals who have heart, compassion, and concern for the world and its people. Socialism is going to conquer the world sooner or later, so if we're smart we'll help it along.

The Jerk was an "intellectual." We knew it because he told us . . . and told us . . . and told us again. Hadn't he spent four years away at college with money enough for tuition, housing, meals, books, and a car to drive to the "Down with America" rallies? Of course, it was all furnished by good ole Mom and Dad who were hard at work in the very same free enterprise system junior was plotting to overthrow. After four years of sacrifice, those hardworking parents watched their offspring march across the stage, sandals and beads under his robe, to receive his degree. "You are now educated!" the college told him. And now here he was—a big-time radio talk show host who knew everything!

The Jerk was convinced the airwaves belonged to him. He saw himself as having been called by some Great Force to preach the gospel of secular humanism and total freedom from Christianity. The moment this man went on the air, he was ready to attack anybody who challenged his cherished beliefs. He sounded as if he had graduated from the "Sam Donaldson Charm School." And should a Christian dare trespass his sanctified airwaves—maybe have the nerve to suggest there might possibly be moral absolutes, even a God—*The Jerk* would make him feel as if he had just crawled out from under a large rock or recently arrived from the distant planet Mongo.

I never heard a conservative or Christian talk show host, only rabid secular humanists. For the life of me, they all sounded as if they were evil little gods shouting from their unholy temples atop some faraway mountains, spouting continuous streams of erratic fulminations against God, Jesus Christ, Christians, conservatives, patriotism, faith, individualism, apple pie, and motherhood—as well as a host of other things they considered to be out of step with the Modern Age.

After listening to all these programmed clones for a while, out of sheer frustration I would slam my fist against the dashboard of my car and say, "Someone needs to speak out! Someone has to give people a way to challenge this propaganda!"

Then came the day I made my decision: I could sit on the sidelines no longer. If no one else would counter this national insanity, I would give it my best shot. Radio would be my medium. I felt it was better for my purposes than television because it's a general rule that on television people's attention can't be held on any one subject longer than about six minutes. I knew it would take longer than that to develop the topics I wanted to bring to light. Anyway, I liked radio. Yes, radio was for me.

And what if the networks closed their doors to my program? What if they denied us use of their facilities? Well, then we would build our own. "Freedom of the press belongs to him who owns one," someone once said. I believed it.

That was the beginning of the "Point of View" radio talk show.

Now here I am, sitting five days a week at the interview table on "Point of View," discussing issues with some of the most informed people our country has to offer. Day after day, week after week, I am constantly amazed at how much I learn. Our listeners who call in tell me they, too, are becoming more and more aware and informed. And because they're more aware and informed, they are becoming more involved. We *are* making a difference!

When I step back and look at how far we've come, it boggles my mind. The conversations among my guests and our listeners and me are now transmitted to three separate satellites stationed in a geostationary orbit 22,300 miles above the earth. "Point of View" is carried on almost three hundred radio stations in the United States, reaches into much of Central and South America and into parts of Europe via shortwave, as well as into Red China over a powerful shortwave radio station, built by George Otis, on the island of Guam. In addition, the program is heard in New Zealand, South Africa, and many other countries by means of tape delay.

Let me tell you something: it's a tremendous responsibility to sit down in that studio each day and hear the announcer say, "And now here's your host, Marlin Maddoux." It's an awesome responsibility to see the engineer give me the signal that my mike is open. It's an unbelievable responsibility to know that several million people are listening to what my guest and I have to say. I do my best to keep from thinking of it in terms of a large audience. To be honest, I'm not that brave.

Over the years I've found I'm happiest and at my best—when I can sit and probe a person who has done the "homework" on a particular subject and then is able to share that information with our listening audience. It is my job as host to help my guest articulate his or her views, to create a climate of friendliness and relaxation so that the guest can be at his or her best.

THE GUEST

After almost twenty years in the broadcast business, and after conducting thousands of interviews, I have learned that some people have trouble simply talking into a microphone. They experience "mike fright." Others, though accustomed to speaking in front of crowds, have trouble with our format because there isn't a live audience out there in front of them.

So it's up to me to draw my guests out, to help them relax and be at their best. It's very important that I not see a guest as an adversary to be ambushed or destroyed. I must approach each one as an intelligent person who has something to share with us.

What a guest needs of me is a good friend, one who is interested in what he or she has to say, one who knows how to listen. Often I find myself totally absorbed in my guests' stories or crusades. The exciting thing is, if I'm interested, I almost always find that the people listening in on the radio are interested as well.

What I do find disturbing is to have a person agree to be on the program—at times even insist on it—and then come to the studio totally uninformed on the subject and unprepared for our interview. I'll never forget a man who once came on and talked about secular humanism in public school textbooks. This fellow had no strong facts and not a single example. Oh, yes, secular humanism was there, he insisted, but he surely couldn't show it to us. I don't want to talk with people about their ideas and opinions; what I want is facts. Facts are what my listeners want, too, and they have a right to them.

I'm afraid I'm not always nice to guests who come to us unprepared. When someone comes in without having the facts together, yet tries to come off as an expert, I press hard. I don't like dishonesty. I've been known to be awfully tough on a person who is trying to sell something "far out" to the audience—or even worse, something that is just plain wrong. And I don't make any apologies for such an interview, either. After all, no one is forced to be on the program.

The approach I take in "Point of View" is that of a one-to-one conversation. I like to think of it as one other person and me sitting together in a coffee shop drinking coffee, just talking about whatever is on our minds. The audience is the guy sitting in the next booth, eavesdropping on our conversation. When he can stand it no longer, he turns around and asks to join us. He then expresses his view on whatever subject we are discussing, or maybe he asks a question of one of us.

THE AUDIENCE

The "guy in the next booth" comes in many forms. That person may be a businessman driving in his car on one of the nation's highways, a farmer on his tractor somewhere in Iowa, a homemaker in Alabama, a judge in Ohio, a preacher in California, or an inmate locked up in any one of the thousands of prisons across the country. And like the guy in the next booth, our program's listeners want to join in and express their views or ask a question. And that's exactly what we want them to do.

To accommodate our listeners, we installed 1-800-number phone lines. Now people can call in from across the nation without having to pay long distance rates. And call in they do! According to a count furnished to us by the phone company, every month thousands of people attempt to call in on the show but aren't able to get through—and that's in addition to all those who *do* talk to us! One day I answered the phone and was greeted by this exclamation: "At last, I'm on!"

"What do you mean?" I asked the woman on the other end of the line.

Her answer: "I've been trying to talk to you for *six years!*"

All I could do was tell her how glad I was she hadn't given up.

A radio talk show is also a lot like listening in on a party line telephone conversation. I remember when my maternal grandmother (we called her "Mama") lived in the country and had an old-fashioned telephone hanging on her wall. It looked like a mahogany box with a crank on the side. When we wanted to make a call, we rang up the telephone operator by turning the little crank. The operator would answer, "Number please." We would give her the number we wanted, and she would put the call through for us.

Mama was on a party line—a telephone line she shared with several other families. When anyone got a call, all the phones on the party line rang. To indicate which call was for whom, the telephone company devised a system of long rings and short rings. Someone might be assigned two long rings, someone else one long and three short. When Mama heard her combination of rings, she would always say, "That's my ring!" and hurry over to answer it.

As the phones rang along the party line, it set in motion a very interesting social phenomenon: When the phone sounded in all the houses, it was answered by the person for whom it was intended; but if the answering person listened very carefully, she could usually hear the faint clicks of receivers all along the party line as the others picked up their own phones and settled in to hear their neighbor's "private" conversation.

A radio talk show is somewhat like a national party line call. When I talk to a person on his or her telephone somewhere across America, people all along the way tune in their radios and eavesdrop on our conversation. It turns into something similar to a town meeting where people can respond immediately to the day's news events or whatever subject we happen to be discussing at the time. Thus the live-by-satellite, nationwide talk show becomes a barometer of how people feel about what's happening in their world. Through it people become friends with people they've never met and probably never will meet.

I owe a great deal to the hundreds of guests I've interviewed over the years. Many of them have been responsible for "educating" me, by making me take a hard look at some of my own ideas about everything from abortion to government. They've challenged me, forcing me into hours of research on a multitude of topics.

Since I'm host, the listeners all get to know me and my family, my strengths, and my shortcomings. When I go to a city to speak and I meet some of our listeners, I'm always a little embarrassed because people speak to me as if we've known each other all our lives. I really would *like* to know them, but I don't. Unfortunately, that's the nature of the mass media.

I owe a great deal to my listeners, and believe me, I take the responsibility seriously. In order to critique myself, I try to listen to two or three program tapes each week. When I'm away from the pressure of being "live" on the air, I'm able to evaluate my own performance as well as those of my guests more objectively.

There are times when I am, admittedly, a bit direct with a caller. I have been known to hang up on someone who was wasting both my time and the audience's with nonsensical palaver. A caller may be thoroughly enjoying the sound of his own voice, and he attempts to run rough-shod over both me and the audience. But the listeners are suffering from collective boredom, and it's my responsibility to keep the show moving along. When someone talks and talks and talks, I wait for him to take a breath; then I take over. I thank him for calling, and he's off the air before he knows what's happening. If I allowed a caller to continue to ramble, I wouldn't be doing my job. A national unrehearsed, spontaneous show such as "Point of View" cannot work unless the host keeps a firm grip on the proceedings.

Ours is not a counseling program. By its very nature it is confrontational. Because we deal with extremely critical issues, it naturally creates tension, friction—sometimes even heated disagreement. You see, we touch people where they live. We disturb their thinking. We challenge their long-cherished beliefs. Sometimes we hit pretty close to home, and some people just cannot stand the pressure.

Because credibility is the very heart of the soul of "Point of View," I never present information I'm not convinced is authentic and correct. Before I go on the air with any story, I'm careful to make sure it comes from a reliable source. If the authenticity of a story is challenged, I go back over my sources to see if, in fact, there was a misrepresentation. If the information is wrong, I am all too willing to correct it on the air. On a few occasions, I've had to do just that.

Radio, you see, isn't like television. Television is an action medium. That's why, for example, the most bizarre, offbeat, and offensive rock groups of our time are the ones that get the air time. They are different, freakish, absurd, and outlandish. But they are "visual," and the networks love them. Media people are not out to promote an organized, civilized society. That's too mundane, too boring. Such a mission wouldn't do a thing to create excitement, so the cameras seek out those who are "out of step" with the majority of the population. Shock serves the purpose of the television camera. Showing a drunk sprawled out on a city street, rather than the millions of hard-working, law-abiding citizens of the nation, is news. As the saying goes: "If dog bites man, that's not news. But if man bites dog—that's news."

If you are to become a discerning individual, able to maintain some degree of intellectual equilibrium, you must understand that the television networks' first and foremost job is to "get the numbers." The company only makes a profit if you and I watch. We are the buying, spending public. How do they attract those "numbers"? Why, by presenting a better show. It makes no difference if that show is called the evening news. It's all the same. It's show business.

Every day and every night of the year we should be questioning a great deal of what we see and hear on television and radio news shows and what we read in newspapers and news magazines. We should ask questions when we hear reports of "radical abortion protesters." We should ask questions when we read articles on sex education and AIDS and gay rights. And we should ask questions when we look over the movie and television choices produced by Hollywood.

Unfortunately few of us ever ask anything at all. We trust our eyes and ears. The interpretation of what we see and read and hear we leave to the "professionals"—the newscasters and the news writers. So most Americans never really know the truth.

Yet you and I want to know the truth. I want to be aware enough to recognize the twisted, the hyped, the misrepresented, the downright lie. But it isn't enough simply to be aware. I want to do something as well. You too? Well, hang on. If you will stay with me through the chapters of this book, I promise you two things: First, you'll learn a lot. (In some areas, I found out more than I ever wanted to know!) Second, you'll find out what you can do to help.

CHAPTER 2

Open Line for Disenfranchised Americans

"We have Ruth from Pennsylvania on the line. You're on the air, Ruth."

"Hello, Marlin. I'm a first-time caller and I just wanted to tell you I agree with everything your guest has said about the junk and slime on TV. Sometimes I think I'm the only one who cares anymore. My kids say I worry too much about the programs they watch and the rock music they listen to."

"I can't imagine worrying too much," I answered.

"Well, it sure is encouraging to hear you say so. My kids say everybody watches that stuff. If it weren't for you and your guests and your listeners who call in, I might believe it. It's so good to know I'm not fighting alone!"

Day after day, week after week, month after month, people like Ruth call in to "Point of View" to comment, argue, ask questions, or simply air their opinions. But it wasn't always that way.

Shortly after making the decision to go on radio, I approached a local station and bought fifteen minutes of daily airtime, Monday through Friday. The format of the program was simple: I would invite a guest each week to appear on the program, and we would tape five fifteen-minute segments to be aired the following week.

Although the response from the audience was good, I

wasn't on the air long enough to build a financial support base. (I got many phone calls and letters but no money.) After a few months I could no longer pay the bills and had to cancel the show.

A few days after I had canceled the program, Joe Willis, the station manager, called. "Would you come in next Monday to interview a celebrity who's coming through town?"

"I'd be happy to," I told him.

I went to the station and interviewed the guest for thirty minutes. When I started to leave the studio, Joe asked, "How about tomorrow? Could you interview another guest we have coming in?"

I told him I would.

After the interview the following day, Joe took me aside. "Marlin," he asked, "would you consider coming in on a regular basis to host our afternoon interview program?"

What could I say? He was offering me the chance to do at no cost what I had been paying him for the privilege of doing.

"I'll be happy to be a regular," I told him, "*if* you will agree to two things. First, give me a free hand in choosing my guests and the topics we'll discuss. I want to have complete editorial control over the program. Second, apply any pay for my work to the balance of the bill I owe the station." In those early days, it was still a part-time enterprise. I really had no plans to make it a full-time job.

The first condition didn't seem to be a problem. Joe had no trouble turning editorial control over to me. The second condition, however, brought a look of agony to his face. Gradually his pained expression subsided, however, and before long, with a broad smile on his face, he offered me his hand, and we shook on it.

And so "Point of View" was born. Because I was determined that my program would not simply slip into the same mold as all those other talk shows across America, I adopted the slogan: "The talk show that's different!" I would sound a different trumpet. I would give the silenced American people a medium through which they could express their views without being treated like scum.

The program originally aired on radio station KDTX in Dallas, Texas, and was carried by that station for several years. When the management decided to change the station's format, we had to look for another station.

We moved to radio station KVTT in Dallas, and for the next several years "Point of View" was carried solely by that station. Then, in 1981, we began simulcasting through a telephone hook-up on radio station KSBJ in Houston, Texas.

The response we got in Houston was both immediate and dramatic. It was as if blinders had been stripped from the eyes of thousands of people. Doctors, lawyers, school teachers, ministers, housewives, students, salesmen— people from all walks of life—wrote to me saying, "Marlin, where have I *been* all my life? I didn't know these things were going on!"

When we covered subjects such as the influence of secular humanism on school children or bias in the media, hundreds of listeners would write in and tell me they had done some checking on their own and, sure enough, what we were saying was correct. The facts had been right there in front of their eyes, but they never saw them until someone pointed them out. The most frequent response was, "Now that I'm informed, what can I do? I want to help wake up America!"

That's when people started telling me that somehow we had to go nationwide with our program. We *had* to rouse America from her sleep before it was too late. It was our responsibility. And so, in a giant leap of faith, we signed a contract to broadcast on satellite.

Our first satellite broadcast was on September 15,

1982. I had no idea how historic that day was to become. Only later did we began to see that we were pioneering a new field in broadcasting. "Point of View" was, in fact, the first conservative issue-oriented radio talk show to broadcast via satellite.

After a slow start, stations across the nation began to pick up the program and carry it. Back in 1982 satellite communication was new, and most of us in the industry knew very little about it. Besides that, the receiving equipment was extremely expensive. Most small "mom and pop" radio stations—and many Christian stations as well—just couldn't afford to install it.

Even so, I knew we had the opportunity to make an "end run" around the major networks. We could get our message out. For the first time since the invention of radio, we had the opportunity to break the monopoly that those who controlled the major networks held over the minds of the American people. There was no choice; we *had* to press forward.

From the beginning we knew it was unlikely we would be able to convince the large, major stations to carry our programming. But there were hundreds of smaller radio stations out there. We figured if we could mobilize them into a mighty, united voice covering the land, we could beat the odds. So, Joel Barnes, my first engineer and salesman—and now news anchor for USA Radio Network—started calling radio stations all across America. He shared our vision with them and asked them to carry our program.

Because satellite broadcasting was new, Joel had a tough time convincing radio stations that a nationwide talk show would draw an audience. Yet, gradually, hard work and gentle persuasion began to pay off; almost weekly the number of stations carrying "Point of View" increased.

At first I'd been quite dubious. I'd thought, *I'll give it a try for ninety days*. By the end of that time, my attitude had changed. *Maybe we're on to something big*, I thought.

I'd better take this satellite thing more seriously. Maybe this is the wave of the future.

I began buying books and magazines about satellite technology. Television was the major application, I learned. Little had been done with the technology for radio. I became so excited that the rest of the staff could hardly contain me. "It's right there!" I told them. "It's at our very fingertips!"

Here before us was the means for reaching the nation. No longer did we have to depend on telephone "land lines" to transmit the signal. Broadcasting by satellite was much less expensive, far more dependable, and of better quality. Everything was in place. All we had to do was seize the opportunity.

One day our engineer was showing me how a satellite transmitter works, trying his best to put it in simple terms so that I could understand. As we stood there, looking at the black boxes and the wiring and the dials and lights, he told me, "Marlin, the technology is there. We have done our part. Now it's up to broadcasters like you to dream the dream, to see the vision of how to use it to reach the world with the truth."

The dream was mine. I had caught the vision. As the technology continued to develop, the cost of the equipment came down in price until it was within reach of even the smallest stations. More affordable receiving equipment for the stations worked to our advantage. These new breakthroughs in satellite broadcasting equipment made the growth of "Point of View" possible.

Now that "Point of View" has been on the air for several years and our number of stations has reached almost three hundred, we're beginning to see that our original calculations were right. The people *are* there. They *do* want to speak, and they want to be heard. When we give them the opportunity to be heard, they take advantage of it—by the tens of thousands!

AMERICANS SPEAK OUT

To the previously silenced millions, talk radio has opened a whole new dimension of freedom of expression. People who for years have felt alone, disenfranchised, and disheartened over conditions in our nation have caught new hope through hearing guests and callers talk on the radio. And being able to voice their own opinions as well has made the experience even more rewarding for them.

"I was concerned about the way our newscasters were welcoming Gorbachev with open arms," a businessman from Atlanta told me. "But I figured I must be the only suspicious person around."

He isn't. Nor is he alone in his feelings of isolation. Thousands of people have written and called in to tell me they had thought they were all alone in their views and convictions. Hearing people from all across America expressing similar thoughts has given them new hope and fresh enthusiasm. It has also given them a conviction. "If we become informed" they say, "and if we join ranks and work together, we *can* effect change in this nation."

"Never again will I be satisfied to teach what I read in the textbooks without sifting and questioning and challenging," wrote a public high school teacher from Boise.

"Marlin, it used to be when I watched the news on television, I believed it all," said an oilman from Houston. "No more. You've taught me how to watch wisely."

As you can see, our callers are a pivotal part of "Point of View." And they are truly a cross section of America. In fact, they *are* America. We get calls from California to New York, from Alaska to Florida, from the bluff of Minnesota to the valley of south Texas.

What we see every day is the American system *working!* We witness true freedom of speech, the first amendment to the Constitution lifted off the page and thrust into action. On "Point of View," people speak their minds, and they do it without fear that the KGB or the Democrats or the Republicans or the FBI or the Internal Revenue Service will come knocking on their doors. This is the American system at its best.

And all the while I get to sit at my interview table and see the names of callers (and the cities they call from) print out across the computer screen in front of me. When our producer answers the telephone, that's all she asks of a caller—first name and the city from which he or she is calling. No one is screened. No one is kept off the air to prevent disagreement with me or my guest. That wouldn't be fair. No, we take the calls as they come.

When I punch the phone line up and announce that the caller is on the air, both our voices go from the broadcast center via microwave to the Dallas Teleport. There they are fed to a satellite 22,300 miles out in space where they are "backhauled" to United Video in Chicago. Then Chicago beams them up to another satellite, another 22,300 miles out in space, then down to radio stations all across the nation. Incidentally, the time lapse between when the caller starts to talk and when listeners hear the voice on the radio is less than *two-fifths of one second*. Now that is space-age technology!

I wish you could be with me during some of the broadcasts. When the subject is important and the guest believes strongly in what he's saying, his passion can be felt all across the nation. Abortion, Soviet influence in Nicaragua, occultism in our public schools, family violence—these are subjects people care about. And when a guest's passion is caught by the listeners, the phones fairly crackle with excitement.

When Betty first called me, she wasn't very friendly. We had been talking about television sitcoms and how they actually preach morals, values, and philosophy through their comedy. "Off the wall" and "a real kook" were two of the phrases Betty used to describe me.

Evidently we had more of an influence on Betty than she cared to admit, for when she called back several weeks later she had this to say: "I started looking at some of the television comedies my kids watch. And you know what my immediate reaction was? I stopped my kids from watching them." Until then, Betty had considered television to be strictly entertainment. No more. Now she monitors the TV watching. "The thing was," she explained, "I started to see where it really was subtly affecting my children. And it scared me."

THE PEOPLE WHO ARE CAUGHT IN THE ISSUES

We at "Point of View" choose our topics carefully. Many of them are subjects about which most people don't even think until they hear them presented in very human, understandable terms. People may not understand lawsuits over the humanistic contents of a public school history book. But they certainly *do* understand the emotional words of a distraught mother who, when she read unbelievable things in her son's textbook, protested to the school principal. When she could get no cooperation there—no one would even listen to her—she charged a bus ticket on her credit card and rode to the state capitol to register her outrage personally.

Listeners understand when that mother tells of the helpless anger and frustration of being in turn ignored, jeered, ridiculed, and threatened. I *know* they understand because when we present such a story on "Point of View," hundreds of people write to say, "Enough is enough. It's time for *me* to get involved!"

Many of us do not understand all the legal or medical jargon surrounding many of our nation's major controversies. Most of us are unable to cut through the incomprehensible newspeak on many issues. But we can understand a young girl who calls in and describes being rushed into an abortion by so-called counselors at an abortion clinic. Our hearts break as we listen to her tearful account of the guilt and anguish, which has become part of her every waking hour.

The thing is that most people's opinions are formed by the reporting they see on television or hear on the radio or read in newspapers and news magazines, however one-sided it may be. Many won't even consider the other side unless and until they hear it presented in human terms that allow them to understand and feel. The result of an emotional, balanced, caring approach to tough subjects is a society in which people are informed, enlightened, instructed, and motivated to action.

And believe me, motivated people do act. The effects of their actions can be felt all the way from their local church congregations to the White House, from their local school boards to the halls of Congress, from their local city councils to the producers of slime television and movies in Hollywood, from local newspapers to the corporate offices of the national businesses that buy time on the national networks to pump such programming into the homes of America. These remote agencies are beginning to feel the impact of the rising voice of the conservative millions. Should they decide to ignore it, it will be at their own peril.

I often receive calls during the program from parents who express shock and outrage at what is being taught in the public schools under the guise of "sex education."

"When the sex ed. program was first presented to our community," said Tom from California, "my wife and I were all for it. We couldn't understand why those radical parents got so upset. Protesting parents went so far as to accuse the school system of being in collusion with people who would like to 'sexually seduce' their children! We couldn't believe it."

Many thousands of parents across America feel just as Tom felt. "Why do a handful of radical parents have to cause so much trouble?" they wonder.

The end of Tom's account is one I've heard over and over again. The oft-repeated story goes something like this: "Mr. Maddoux, when I finally took the time to take a hard look at what they were teaching my child, I was outraged." Most parents go on to explain how difficult they found it to lay their hands on the textbooks, workbooks, filmstrips, and—hardest of all—the teachers' manuals for the courses.

One sincere parent from Florida told me, "I went to the public school officials for the sole purpose of being reassured that what these 'Christian' parents were saying wasn't true."

When she got there, however, she ran up against a stone wall. "The teachers and school administration treated me as if I was a nobody with no right even to look into the files of my own children. They made me feel uninformed, like I was too stupid to know what was best for my own kids."

So she took her questions to the school board. But she fared no better there. "I was treated like a troublemaker," she told me. "Everyone was so hostile!"

By this time our Florida caller knew something was terribly wrong. She was facing her own local Watergate-type cover-up. Not about to give up, she gave the school board fair warning that she would be at the next public board meeting, and she would be demanding answers. She had contacted no organizations, nor was she a front for any group of people. She was simply a concerned parent who thought she was confronting a problem unique to her school district.

Imagine her amazement when she arrived at the school board meeting and encountered television cameras from three local stations.

"Why were they there?" I asked her.

"To record what one called my imbecilic prattling," she answered.

What followed during the next few weeks, our caller

told us, was a barrage of publicity, all of it extremely negative. "They accused me of being a plant for various right-wing groups out to destroy pluralism in our nation," she told us. In spite of being belittled and ridiculed in the newspapers, on local talk shows, and on television, she stuck to her guns and continued to fight for her rights and the rights of her children.

After listening to her story, all I could say was, "Welcome, dear, to World War III."

Skirmishes in this war sometimes even involve rights we consider to be guaranteed by the First Amendment to the Constitution.

THE NEBRASKA CASE

Religious freedom. We all have it, right? If you believe that, read on.

Several years ago I began getting reports from various sources that there was a Baptist pastor in Nebraska who had been thrown in jail for operating a school in his church. The first few times I heard about it, I dismissed it as too bizarre to be true. After all, this is America, the land of freedom. Maybe in Russia, but that kind of thing couldn't happen here in the good old U.S. of A. Why, our country has a constitutional amendment guaranteeing that the government will stay out of the work and ministry of the church. If education isn't a fulfillment of Christ's commission to the church, then what is?

But the reports persisted, so I finally felt compelled to investigate. What I found appalled me. Religious persecution does happen right here in America.

Not only was the pastor in question thrown in jail, I found, but the students had been dragged out of the church and some of their parents were also in jail.

Their crime? Operating a school, as part of the church's ministry, without benefit of a license from the state. Talk about dangerous criminals!

When I got into this issue, once again some of my long-held assumptions and beliefs came into question. I had to ask myself, "Is it right and proper for the government to hold a monopoly on the education of our children?" I mean, why should a Christian parent be forced by the power of the state to send a child to a school that is gong to undermine that young person's Christian faith?

When a child's parents and church teach her that she is the product of creation by a loving God and then her teacher tells her she is the product of mindless chance—evolution, they call it—conflicting ideas and values she is not mature enough to handle are set up within that child's mind. Is this really something that should be forced upon her?

As I continued my investigation into this story, it seemed to me that the state was attempting to fill the role not only of educator, but also of parent. The state was telling parents they didn't have the right to teach their children religious values. Instead, they were required to expose their children to a multiplicity of values, then let them choose for themselves which ones are for them.

Now, the very idea of the state exposing children to many different values, it seemed to me, presupposes that the state has the right to violate parents' wishes for their children's moral and religious development.

When I finally went on the air with the Nebraska church-school story, the reaction from the listening audience was one of absolute outrage. Parents, pastors, business people, and concerned citizens alike wrote to tell me how they felt. But that's not all they did. Many of them went to Nebraska to protest in person the treatment of this pastor and his church.

There is a footnote to this story: the state of Nebraska, as the result of the mounting pressure and uproar over the issue, passed new laws that got the state off the backs of parents who opted to put their children in private church schools.

Millions of Americans are saying, "Enough!" They are challenging the so-called "sexperts" at school board meetings, in the press, and in the courts of justice.

Our callers are great. Oh, we get an occasional kook. But for the most part, our callers restore our faith in the intelligence, sophistication, and concern of the American people.

Thank you, callers. We couldn't do it without you!

What Ever Happened to the Fun in the Funnies?

Remember when you got up on Sunday morning and spread the brightly colored funny papers out on the living room floor? The smell of breakfast was coming from the kitchen, and your dad was reading the part of the paper he called the "news," and you couldn't understand why grown-ups found that part of the paper so interesting. Remember how—lying there on your stomach, your elbows on the floor and your chin resting in the palms of your hands—you would chuckle at the antics of Joe Palooka or the Katzenjammer Kids or Popeye or Smilin' Jack or Beatle Bailey?

And, if you're like me, even after you grew older and started to read the "news" part of the newspaper, you always knew the way to escape the serious world for a few moments was to flip over to the funnies. You wouldn't find any "serious" cartoons there. They were reserved for the editorial section.

But no more. Now the comics section comes laden with strips that no newspaper should place there. Those strips are not comics. At best they are editorial cartoons; at worst they are liberal propaganda pieces.

And the favorite targets for ridicule in these "cartoons"? You guessed it—conservatives, American institutions, religion in general, and Christians and Christianity in particular. (Cartoon attacks, by the way, are very effective in raising the level of prejudice, animosity, and intolerance against their victims.)

Now, the editorial cartoon is an extremely effective and legitimate method of getting a message across. It has been used for hundreds of years. In the hands of people who understand how to use them, satire and ridicule and humor are potent psychological weapons. Whenever a message is presented in a humorous manner, as is often the case in editorial cartoons, a person's normal conscious defenses are bypassed. Then, with his or her defenses relaxed, that person's subconscious mind is opened to receive and store the "message" sent.

Humor is a way to get around reason and intelligence, a way to appeal indirectly to a person's predilection for prejudice against people who hold different ideas and values. In this process, there is an attempt to create a caricature of the person that is so ridiculous the person will not be taken seriously.

I get more than a little burned up when political cartoonists try to palm their work off as entertainment. They do this, in my opinion, when they attempt to pass their work off as "funnies" and run it in the comics section of the newspaper.

In my estimation one of the biggest perpetrators of this cartoon deception is Garry Trudeau, author of a so-called "comic strip" called *Doonesbury*, which appears in newspapers all across America. Even though it is billed as a "comic strip," it doesn't qualify, in my opinion, to be placed in the comics section of any newspaper. It's an editorial cartoon at best and a platform for Mr. Trudeau's left-of-center political opinions at worst.

Through the clever—and sometimes very entertaining—use of satire, ridicule, and sick humor, Mr. Trudeau denigrates conservatives, traditional values, religion, and patriotism.

Oh, yes, he also regularly parrots the liberal agenda. For example, Mr. Trudeau has constantly attempted to undermine the Nicaraguans who fought against the repressive Communist regime in their country. I consider his April 12, 1987, strip to be one of the most offensive things I've ever seen in print. The subject was a congressional committee hearing in Washington where they were listening to testimony from one of Nicaragua's freedom fighters.

The last frame of the strip showed two freedom fighters holding smoking automatic weapons. One soldier was saying, "I got one! I got a Communist!" The other soldier answered, "Maybe two. She looks pregnant."

The clear purpose of this cartoon was to present the freedom fighters as murderers of innocent people—even pregnant women. Mr. Trudeau didn't bother to show that Nicaragua has become a massive staging area for the Soviets in their quest for world domination. Nor did he show that the Communist regime has imposed a Soviet-style dictatorship over the Nicaraguan people, suppressing human rights and basic freedoms.

Political satire is a legitimate tool, and it has its place. But its place is not in the comic section of our Sunday newspapers. The funnies just aren't funny anymore.

For the past several years, when reading Gary Trudeau's cartoons, I have on occasion had the distinct feeling that he, like so many others in our national media, is trapped in a mental and emotional "time warp" of the 1960s. Why, he even speaks lovingly of the days of "Woodstock" and the "flower children" and other aberrations from intelligent behavior.

But Mr. Trudeau reached an all-time low with his May 7, 1987, strip in which he portrayed President Reagan as a takeoff on the idiotic computer-created television character Max Headroom. Mr. Trudeau showed two men in front of their television set listening to this character engaging in some inane chatter. But in the third panel, Trudeau did a most distasteful thing. He gave the Max Headroom character—President Reagan—this line: "That re-re-reminds me! Kids! Need rock-solid information on 'Safe Sex'? Call this number on your screen."

On the panel below the character was a telephone number. Normally I would have ignored the number, but it caught my eye because it gave a legitimate area code—202. That, I knew, was the Washington, D.C., area code. So, I picked up the phone and dialed the number. A lady answered: "The White House."

I was stunned. "Are you kidding?" I said. "Do you know where I got this number?"

Yes, she said. She was already aware of the strip, and I must say she was commendably cordial under the circumstances.

After I hung up, I tried to get Mr. Trudeau's telephone number. I was sure he would love to get several thousand phone calls from the listeners of "Point of View" commending him on his mindless antics. Unfortunately, I was unable to get it. Pity.

The strip—which was similar to something out of the perverse movie *Animal House* or other such tasteless buffoonery—was either an imbecilic prank by a man with an adolescent sense of humor, or else it was a very effective method of harassing and injuring someone with whom he disagreed. Personally, I don't think Mr. Trudeau is an adolescent. Neither do I think the American people—most of whom have a keen sense of fair play—upon reflection see it as being funny.

Mr. Trudeau's behavior reminds me of the teenage boy who writes unkind things—and the phone number—of the girl who jilted him. Where? Why, on the restroom wall at his high school!

When I discovered I couldn't find Mr. Trudeau's telephone number, I decided to do the next best thing. I called the *Dallas Times-Herald,* asked for the editorial department, and told them I felt the strip was at an all-time low, even for Garry Trudeau. I also told them newspapers all across America were showing courage and a sense of fair play by putting the strip where it belonged—on the editorial page instead of in the comic section.

TELEVISION SITCOMS

This same liberal agenda is reflected in the entertainment programs shown nightly on national television.

The term *media* includes many forms of communication, all of which can be used for good or for bad. It all depends on who is controlling them. When we think of entertainment, most of us think in terms of such things as the movies, theater, television, dramas, and situation comedies. Yet there are others who perceive these "entertainments" for what they are—pulpits, platforms from which to preach moral, religious, and political ideas and values.

The entertainment industry is indeed having an effect on the American culture. Unfortunately, too many who can recognize the bias and abuses in the press don't understand that the very same kinds of abuses occur in television programs and in the movies. They just aren't quite so apparent.

Millions of Americans position themselves in front of their television sets each evening to be "entertained." What they don't realize is that they are handing themselves over to master manipulators. With their conscious defenses down, their subconscious minds are wide open to receive impressions, values, moral judgments, and new prejudices—and to be "programmed" in whatever way the brain trust of the media chooses. Of course, it's all done in a most "entertaining" way. And, by the way, at the cost of millions of dollars.

A person can be programmed to adopt an entirely new set of values simply by having his mind bombarded with

slanted, cleverly designed movies, dramas, situation comedies, "documentaries," and other forms of media presentations. And all the time that person will argue that he is not
being affected by them.

This, of course, is the cleverest and most deadly persuasion of all—burying the "message" as unobtrusively as
possible in the medium. That way, you see, the person will
argue that the conclusions he has reached are his own, not
someone else's.

In *The View from Sunset Boulevard,* Ben Stein said:
"In television, the producers and writers are the creative
kings. What they say is law, and that law is transmitted on
the airwaves into millions of homes. Television is not a mir-
ror of anything besides what those few people think." He
further asserted that these same powerful people are deliberately using our most powerful communications medium
to promote "their own social and political views."[1]

Once I began to analyze the subtle—and sometimes
not so subtle—messages contained in the television programs viewed nightly by millions of Americans, it all began
to come into clear focus. It's similar to the little magazines
we used to read when we were in school. There would be
pictures of scenes such as lakes and trees with a caption
instructing us to try to find the hidden animals. At first
glance, we didn't see any animals. But as we concentrated,
the animals began to come into focus. Here we would see a
fish in a tree, there a bird under the water. We didn't see
them at first because our logic told us birds didn't live in the
water and fish didn't live in trees, so subconsciously we
were precluded from looking for such things.

The writers and producers of the television programs
know that you and I are not predisposed to look for political
or social or moral "messages" in the dramatic programs or
situation comedies we watch. That very knowledge gives
them a tremendous avenue for persuasion. Unfortunately,
millions of Americans are being persuaded, molded, and

brainwashed by something they believe to be innocent information or simple entertainment.

I don't think most Americans have yet fully grasped the awesome power of persuasion held by the people who skillfully use television. Nor do they understand that this power is being systematically used to undermine the religious faith of the people of our country.

Dr. James Hitchcock, noted historian and professor of history at St. Louis University, said:

> Television has been by far [secular humanism's] chief disseminator. It would be almost impossible to overestimate its influence. . . . Just as destructive as its concentration on what is deviant and amoral has been television's general ignoring of religion as a positive force. . . . When providing viewers with fictional images of what life is like, television rarely adverts to the fact that, for a great majority of Americans, religious beliefs are an integral part of their lives.
>
> Religiously movitated characters are likely to be neurotics for whom religion is a form of sickness. Rarely are sympathetic characters presented whose lives are strengthened by prayer or the guidance of clergy. Millions of Americans attend church on Sunday and pray in their homes, but rarely are they shown doing this on television.[2]

When the Reverend Donald E. Wildmon, head of the American Family Association, was my guest on "Point of View," he lashed out at television by saying, "Censorship against Christians by network television is so complete that _not one_ continuing series set in a modern day setting has a _single person_ who is identified as a Christian. . . . In fact, when Christians are depicted in programs with a modern day setting, they nearly always are stereotyped as being hypocrites, liars, cheats, frauds. Name one network program, set in a modern day context, which has depicted a Christian as a warm, loving, intelligent, compassionate human being."[3]

I wasn't able to accept Mr. Wildmon's challenge. Such a network show just didn't seem to exist. The censorship against Christians is that complete.

"Me?" you might ask. "Brainwashed by nightly television? Impossible!" You would be surprised. Actually, in the hands of one who understands the technique, it's a rather simple process. You'll be shown a situation or a philosophy or a moral decision played out night after night on national television—especially on the myriad of idiotic situation comedies thrown at you every night of the week. The names and faces may change from season to season, but the messages and techniques remain the same.

Basically, three steps are used in formulating dramatic presentations or these little moral sermonettes we have come to know as sitcoms.

First, the writers and producers "create a situation." It may be, for example, two girls and a boy sharing the same apartment, with all the possibilities such a predicament presents. This was the situation for "Three's Company," a charming little sitcom filled with all kinds of sexual innuendo and suggestive twists and snickering misunderstandings.

Second, they "create tension" between conflicting values in trying to find a solution for the problem or situation. The unfolding of the "tension" phase can go on endlessly. This phase usually takes up most of the program.

Third, they "select the solution" that best expresses the value they want you to embrace as your own morally "right" choice. After examining various moral choices, the characters arrive at the one choice that expresses the value system of the people behind the show. This is all done in such a logical, entertaining way that the viewer nods in agreement that the choice was indeed the proper one.

Through it all, the viewer has unknowingly filed the whole episode away in the subconscious mind to be recalled when he faces a similar situation. And so, a new value has been introduced and passively accepted by the unsuspecting viewer.

When Don Wildmon, made one of his many guest appearances on "Point of View," he told us that a very powerful example of this technique was illustrated in a CBS program called "Not in Front of the Children," aired on October 26, 1982. Here's how Dr. Wildmon described its promotion: "She's living with the man she loves. Now her ex-husband's revenge could cost her the children."

The show itself centered around a mother who invited her lover to move in with her and her two small daughters. Sound interesting? Let's eavesdrop for a bit:

EX-HUSBAND: Why didn't you tell me you were planning to have a man move in here?"

EX-WIFE: I didn't think it was any of your business.

EX-HUSBAND: You didn't think it was my business . . . if my daughters are living in an atmosphere of promiscuity?

EX-WIFE: Living with one man doesn't constitute promiscuity. And besides, they are *our* daughters.

EX-HUSBAND: Nancy, you are the person they respect most in the whole world, and you're teaching them that intimacy outside of marriage is not a sin.

EX-WIFE: I don't think it is. One of the terms of our divorce is that they can go to church with you on Sundays. They have the opportunity to hear your beliefs.

EX-HUSBAND: But all the sermons in the world can't compete against what you're teaching them right here at home.

EX-WIFE: I am being honest with them. I am doing what's right for me, and later on they can do what's right for them.

EX-HUSBAND: If you deliberately choose to have a relationship with some man, that's your right and your choice, even if I don't approve. But what about their rights? They didn't choose to live with this man.

EX-WIFE: I asked them. They wanted to.

EX-HUSBAND: They're babies! They don't know what it means. I forbid you to flaunt this relationship in front of my children!

[Husband leaves. Little girl who has overheard conversation comes in:]

LITTLE GIRL: Mom, are you going to hell?

EX-WIFE: No, sweetheart, I'm not. This is kind of hard to explain. . . . Everyone has their own beliefs. And your daddy thinks the way we're living together is wrong. He has a right to think that. But I don't. I believe God is love, and that's what we have together. Paul [her live-in lover] and I [inspirational music starts again] and you two girls, that's love. And I think God understands that. That's what I believe. And when you two girls are grown up, then you have a right to decide what's right for you. Okay?

LITTLE GIRL: Okay. I knew God wouldn't send you to hell. [Music intensifies]

Then in his soft Mississippi drawl, Don Wildmon said, "Marlin, the remainder of the program is a study in contrasts. At one end of the spectrum is the harsh, bigoted, dogmatic, intolerant, domineering, ill-tempered, biased, overbearing Christian ex-husband. On the other side is the sympathetic, caring, kind, affectionate, gentle, understanding, tender, benevolent, Prince Charming, the secular live-in lover."

Throughout the program, the injured party is the teary-eyed ex-wife who is consistently a victim of Christian intolerance.

In the end, the court finds in favor of the ex-husband, and only a last ditch decision to get married to her lover keeps the children in the mother's home. Everyone lives happily ever after—everyone, that is, except those whose chief defect is their Christian faith. But then the drama leaves the distinct impression that they got what was coming to them.

Then Dr. Wildmon stated the obvious: "The clear teaching of the movie is that humanism is preferable to Christianity."

When the dialogue is put down in cold type and read without the sweet, loving facial gestures of the actors and the "hearts and flowers" violin music, the producer's objective becomes clear. Can any intellectually honest person deny that this little piece of trash is intended to convey a definite message—that Christian morals should be relegated to a long-dead past and that the "New Morality" is far more desirable?

When the writers and producers put the truth into the mouth of a scoundrel or bigot, they know what will happen. We viewers will associate that truth with the character, and we'll reject them both. At the same time, they put their "message" into the mouth of a tender, loving, caring character, knowing that we will embrace not only the character, but the message as well.

This is the method Norman Lear used with such force in the television shows "All in the Family" and "Diff'rent Strokes." Truth, patriotism, and traditional values, for example, were often voiced by "All in the Family" character, Archie Bunker. But Archie is an ignorant bigot, so it's only natural to assume that anything he says is to be rejected. In this same manner Norman Lear often ridicules Christianity, patriotism, the American flag, traditional morality, and conservatives in general. And because he hides his prejudices behind the mask of "comedy," he gets away with it.

But the fact is, "All in the Family" is Norman Lear's own personal pulpit from which he can preach his secular humanist doctrine and ridicule Christianity without being branded a bigot. In the hands of an expert, you see, satire and ridicule are very effective methods of persuasion. And make no mistake about it: Mr. Lear *is* an expert.

Have you seen "My Two Dads"? Now there is a cute little comedy. It has as its premise an adolescent girl whose unmarried mother has died. Because Mom had been intimate with two men—one an archconservative, the other a "hang-loose" artist—she wasn't sure which was her daughter's real father. So guess what she did? She stipulated in her will that the daughter be raised by *both* men. Isn't that sweet? Now the young teenager and her deceased mother's two very different lovers are a cute, funny, happy family.

It is programs like these—repeated dozens of times each week—that cause "moral confusion" in the minds of millions of men, women, and children who watch them. Viewers begin to believe this insistence that biblical truth and morality could be, after all, just a bit restrictive. And, furthermore, maybe Christians really are being more than a little "intolerant" of other people's behavior simply because of their different beliefs. Why, that's un-American, isn't it?

Christians subjected to such programs over a long period of time begin to doubt their own "narrow-minded" moral values. They become increasingly desensitized to such things as adultery, abortion, homosexuality, murder, rape, incest, lesbianism, and a host of other practices the Bible clearly condemns. And when they are sufficiently desensitized, their outrage against such things turns into "tolerance." And, gradually, tolerance turns into approval.

The next step in this moral rape is actually to embrace evil. Over and over again, we have seen this progression of moral manipulation. The Christian becomes so morally confused that nothing in itself seems evil any longer. He now accepts the premise that there are only differing value systems of equal validity and that each person should accept all points of view. In this subtle way, the voice of righteous outrage is being silenced in our society.

HOW THEY DO IT

According to long-time journalist Charles Wiley, it's not hard for a journalist to influence the news. "I'll tell you some of the main ways it's done," he told us on "Point of View." "Then when you read newspapers or listen to the radio or watch television, you'll be able to quickly spot the techniques.

"First of all," he told us, "You should know that lying is one of the least of the problems. There really isn't much of that. Most journalists are too honorable to lie outright. Also, it's not too effective. If you lie, you see, you're likely to get caught, and if you get caught, you lose all credibility."

Having said that, he went into some of the methods journalists do employ:

—The first method is selective coverage.

This is where journalists cover one story and don't cover another one. Or they cover some aspects of a story, and they don't cover other aspects.

A good example of this can be seen in a memo from inside the media. Richard Harwood, the ombudsman of the *Washington Post*, whose job is to monitor the performance of the paper on a daily basis and deal with complaints from readers, criticized his paper for the one-dimensional report in a memo in 1971, which was published in the book, *Of the Press, by the Press, and Others Too.*

[Unfortunately, there were no sequels to this publication so we don't know what the ombudsman has been saying since 1976, the last revision of the book.] Here's what Harwood had to say:

"One of the serious and persistent weaknesses of this newspaper is the one-dimensional report, the tendency to deal with the phenomena of our time through the eyes of a single beholder. It is as if we were to seek the whole reality of the thirties from the movie tales of Bonnie and Clyde. That tendency often produces fascinating visions of the world in which we live. But often, too, they are private, distorted visions that give us no real clutch on reality and make us vulnerable to the charges of superficiality and bias that float around in our ears.

"ITEM: Our long Sunday takeout on Catholic radicals tells us that they are a tiny fragment of the 47 million Catholics in America but their activities 'have sent shock waves throughout the church.' We are given an 88-glimpse of the radicals through their own eyes and through the eyes of three non-radical sympathizers. We are not given a glimpse of the radical movement through the eyes of, say, Knights of Columbus. And that is all the more surprising since the movement's significance is related to the 'shock' it has caused other Catholics.

"One suspects that the Berrigans and other radicals may be, like Abbie Hoffman and Jerry Rubin, little more than media figures; we have certainly done our part to make them household names. But one can't know that if the only view of the movement we get is the view of the radicals themselves. Could it be that they speak for the Catholic majority? Isn't that a significant question to ask about this phenomenon?

"It is our failure to explore the Other Dimension that led, I think, to some of the hysterical coverage of the 'radical movement' on campus and that has led to other journalistic excesses in recent years. One can cite, for example, our extensive reportage on the abortion question which has led some people—myself included—to assume that there is a mass movement in America to enact very liberal abortion laws. It came as something of a surprise to discover in *Science* magazine that every public opinion survey of the past 10 years shows that opposition to liberal abortion laws is far more widespread and deep-seated than, say, opposition to the war in Vietnam; and to discover that this opposition is strongest—hold on to your hat—among women under 30.

You would never know that from reading the *Washington Post*.

"If it is our function as a newspaper to be 'trendy,' to pick up, exploit and promote every fad that comes along, then the points made here are irrelevant. But if it is our function, in that great phrase of Rebecca West's, to "set the face of the age" as it is—not as we would like it to be—then we would do well to look at our performance more carefully."[4]

—Positive/negative coverage is another method.

Here journalists cover some causes and some people positively while they cover others negatively.

—Another method is to play up the positive in one case—the good points, the successes—while playing down the bad points and the failures.

This really shows up in the questions journalists choose to pose to "positive" people ("it's batting practice pitch time, nice and easy, right down the center of the plate") as opposed to those posed to "negative" people ("they plod and probe until they find a flaw; then they go right for the throat").

—The next element is repetition.

In this technique journalists take some stories and report them over and over and over again until no one wants to hear about them any more. The Iran-Contra affair is a good example of this.

—Another method is a lack of perspective.

Journalists report things, but even when they're telling you the truth, they're not really giving you the story because they don't put it into a context that makes any sense.

An illustration of this is a joke that has been making the rounds in Washington: "President Reagan called a press conference at the banks of the Potomac River. When all the reporters got there, including the reporter from the *Washington Post* (the *Post* doesn't like Reagan very much), the president took off his shoes and socks and walked right across the top of the water to the other side of the river.

Then he turned around and walked back. The next day the *Washington Post* ran a headline that read: 'Reagan Can't Swim.'" That's what we mean when we talk about perspective.

—The worst (that means the most effective) is simply the use of semantics.

One of the best examples of this, and one you will see almost any day of the week, is the choice of descriptive words. "In journalism school we were taught to avoid loaded words. We were taught there were certain words that were only to be used when they were the exact word to describe the situation. Now journalists use those words endlessly.

"Here's an example of how it works: I could be here on this show and Marlin might ask me to tell a bit about myself, so I might say, 'I've been a journalist for thirty years.' Now, a newspaper could pick that up and report: 'Charles Wiley said he has been a journalist for thirty years.' That's fact. Just straight reporting. Or the reporter could say, 'Marlin's guest *admitted* he's been a journalist for thirty years.' Or he can say, 'He has *conceded* he's been a journalist for thirty years.' Or he could go to the final step and say, 'Wiley *confessed* he's been a journalist for thirty years.' You see how one word changes the whole meaning."[5]

Remember, we're talking about news reporters here, not about commentators. Commentators have a right to give opinions and draw conclusions and ask questions that reflect the commentator's point of view.

The ombudsman at the *Post* points out another journalistic excess, the error of the biggest and the smallest. Charles Seib, the paper's second ombudsman, says it this way:

Mssrs. Bradlee/Simons   3/10/75
Here's a law to go next to Murphy's: As soon as you print that something is the biggest, smallest, oldest, youngest, richest, poorest or any other-est, someone is certain

to come up with something that is bigger, smaller, older, younger, richer, poorer, etc.

This morning a reader called to say that we were wrong in calling Greenwood's the oldest major black-owned firm in the district in today's paper. He cited these as examples of firms that were older and as large or larger: Hagan's Management Corp., John P. Stewart Funeral Home, Jarvis Funeral Home, McGuire Funeral Home.

He may be wrong, of course. In any case, those words "one of the" are awfully handy unless you've got the superlative absolutely pinned down.

Charlie Seib[6]

An extension of the "law of the biggest and smallest" is the use of words such as *all, every, none, never,* and *always.* A reporter had better have all the facts before making such an assertion.

A friend watched Ken Woodward, religion editor for *Newsweek* magazine, make this mistake on Ted Koppel's "Nightline" during the Jim Bakker scandal. When asked about the recent misappropriation of funds by television evangelists, Woodward said, "All of the television evangelists misappropriate funds."

My friend thought, *All of them?* She knew how many television evangelists there are in the country, besides the well-known national figures.

But Ted Koppel didn't ask Woodward, "Do you really mean all? Do you have proof that every television evangelist in the country has misappropriated funds?"

Instead the viewer was left with the misinformation: all television evangelists have misappropriated the money of innocent Americans.

When you are watching the news on television or reading the paper, become an ombudsman yourself. Look for these discrepancies in news coverage. Monitor the double-think in America for yourself, and decipher the truth behind the prejudice.

In the book *Mediaspeak,* author Donna Woolfolk Cross says,

> There is a growing body of evidence that long-term exposure to the language of TV news is detrimental to a person's thought processes. Seven out of ten people get their information about the world exclusively from television. Yet one recent study revealed that these people can no longer give even one reason to justify their choice of a particular political candidate or policy.[7]

When Dr. Larry Poland, author of *The Last Temptation of Hollywood,* was on "Point of View," a man by the name of Jason called from Virginia. "What angers me," Jason said, "is that Christians are going to movie houses. I don't think we have any business seeing the things they show."

"I agree with his very well-placed concern about Christians consuming things that are grossly destructive to the Christian life," Dr. Poland answered. "I'm very concerned and angry about the statistics from national surveys by the Gallup organization and others that indicate that there is no statistically significant difference between the number of hours of television watched, or the programs watched, by those who profess to be born-again Christians."

So one thing we can do—if we are truly concerned—is to stop consuming the junk they are putting out.

1. Turn Off the TV

When we discuss the effects of television on "Point of View," many people call in from all across America and say they have opted to throw the television out of their homes and live without it. In my opinion, any family with small children should carefully consider this option. For television, you see, is the most persuasive, seductive form of mass communication in America today. And it has almost totally saturated our society.

Tragically, Americans tend to trust anything that comes over television. TV is so influential, in fact, that if something in society fails to live up to the image portrayed on the screen, there is an almost immediate effort to make society conform to the image. Is it any wonder then that young people of the TV generation won't tolerate anyone who dares challenge their ideas of truth, wisdom, style, and acceptable behavior?

Because the mass media are so adept at disguising the fact that they are being used to promote the anti-Christian, secular humanistic worldview, people are not successfully defending themselves against propaganda. They aren't even aware they are being propagandized. After years of such propaganda coming from the television, the movies, the arts and literature, and the schools and universities, the American people are marching lockstep to the tune played by the propagandists.

Said Dr. Poland, "I think we are being adjusted and manipulated a quarter turn at a time to a pagan worldview by so much consumption of films and television. The body of Christ across America needs to say, 'Enough, already!' and draw the line and say, 'We're not going to patronize the trash that comes from these sources of media anymore,' that we are just asking for trouble."

The first thing you can do is discipline your own television watching. The next thing is to set some rules for your family's watching as well.

But you likely want to go beyond your own family's watching habits. You want to make a difference in our society. It is possible, you know. Others have done it.

Take Terry Rakolta, for instance. Mrs. Rakolta, a suburban Detroit mother of four, was shocked when she saw an episode of the sitcom "Married . . . with Children" on the Fox television network. What she was expecting was fun family entertainment. What she got was disgusting Fox filth: off-color humor, sexual brashness, and gutter language all played out in the setting of a man and woman at home with their teenage daughter and adolescent son.

That episode so startled Terry Rakolta that she determined to take action. After intensely monitoring several weekly episodes, she began an equally intensive letter-writing campaign. Who did she write to? Brilliantly, she directed her letters to the show's sponsors. She told them of her shock at the program and exactly what it was she objected to.

Can you guess what happened? Terry Rakolta's letters worked. At least three major advertisers decided to pull their advertising from "Married . . . with Children." Coca-Cola said they might do the same, at least on those episodes they deemed offensive.

Because of the outstanding response, Mrs. Rakolta's cleanup crusade itself made news. The national press, no less, picked up the story, and she was interviewed on at least one major network news show.

Best of all, Terry Rakolta's efforts—and the response she got—should be an inspiration to every one of us.

Do you sometimes think nothing can be done to clean up television? Do you shrug your shoulders in resignation and say, "It's a useless battle. Why fight? I sure can't do anything single-handedly." If so, think of Terry Rakolta and what she accomplished.

2. Write Letters

Terry Rakolta isn't alone. Across America common, everyday people—people no different from you—are starting to speak out individually. And they are starting to get things done.

A listener, an employee of a television station, called in and told me, "We ran a show that was a bit more daring than what we usually play and we got two letters of complaint. So the manager ordered the show canceled. He explained it to us by saying, 'We canceled the program because of the flood of opposition mail.' We got two letters, and to him it was a flood!"

Anyone who works in the broadcast media knows very well how much difference just one or two letters can make. A hundred telephone calls may not provoke a station or show to change what they're doing, but just a handful of sincere, heartfelt letters can completely change the direction for a broadcast outlet.

Letters, you see, speak loudly. And it makes sense. Because radio and television stations must keep their letters on public file, several letters complaining about a show—or a station as a whole, for that matter—will often result in action. And letters of complaint to program sponsors hit sponsoring companies where it hurts most—right in the pocketbook.

The people who have brought about change through their letter writing will tell you two things. First, they're often surprised by the response they get. And second, they are glad they spoke out.

Jane Chastane, the author of the book *I'd Speak Out on the Issues—If I Only Knew What to Say,* told us, "The really difficult part is to take that first step. I had the Roper Institute run a survey of all the polls that have been taken asking the question: 'Have you ever written a letter to one of your elected representatives?' This covered polls taken over the past ten years. What we found was that the highest percent who said they ever wrote a letter was 20 percent. (The pollsters tell me this is very high because people will lie to those taking the polls. They think, 'Well, I'm going to write a letter. In fact, I'm going to write it tonight. So actually if they'd asked me this tomorrow, the answer would be "yes," so I'm going to say, "yes." ')

"But the polls show it this way: 20 percent say they have written. Another 20 percent don't care; they would never even be interested. But the other 60 percent answered the same way year after year: 'I'm getting ready to do it.'"

Writing a letter is an excellent way to have your opinion heard. But good intentions mean nothing. You have to get down and do the writing.

So how do you write a letter that will have impact?

"When you get right down to it," Jane Chastane told us, "there are only two kinds of information, facts and opinions. The beautiful thing about using facts is that they're incontestable, they're indisputable, and they're noncontroversial. A fact is a fact. And it only takes two or three facts to make a good letter."

3. Monitor Your TV

Dr. Billy Melvin is a man you would enjoy knowing. As chairman of CLEAR-TV he not only monitors what is shown on American television, but he plays a vital role in the massive movement to clean up what's already on. Other Americans are joining Dr. Melvin; some run these monitoring groups from their homes, making tapes available to listeners of local television stations.

Recently Dr. Melvin sent us a clipping from the *New York Times* saying that when ABC Television tried to round up sponsors for their special show, "Crimes of Passion II," they came up zip! Not one single advertiser was willing to put its product on the line for a show which featured reenactments of gory crimes, including two stabbings, a shooting, and a man setting fire to his wife.

The *Times* said that "one network executive, who asked not to be identified, said, 'A logical person could assume that the advertisers were afraid of the monitoring.'"

We asked Dr. Melvin if we are finally beginning to see the erosion of advertising support on trash TV. He said, "Over the last three years that we have been working with these corporations, I have discovered that there are a number of them who were trying to be responsible in the placement of their advertising. In other words, they were already concerned about trends in prime-time television programming. CLEAR-TV has served to encourage them in their stand."

"What can Americans do to help clean up television?" I asked him.

"The only thing I know of that is really effective is to write a letter to the corporate sponsor of a specific program," he told us. "It's only since we got to the sponsors that we have gotten action."

A caller who wished to remain anonymous (I called him Joe) telephoned "Point of View" one day. "I work in management for a television station," he told us. "I thought you should know that there is a very powerful method of telling a television station that you do or do not appreciate the programming you're seeing on that station. Most people don't realize it, but stations are required to keep a public file of letters that people send to television stations. This is reviewed at license renewal time. Stations, you see, are required by their licenses to serve the community to which they broadcast."

Your letters do matter! If you write the sponsor, the money source will be hurt. If you write the station, it will become a matter of public record.

"I have heard managers say in meetings," Joe told us, " 'We will go just as far as the public will let us go.' "

If they go too far, whose fault is it anyway?

MOVIES

In 1988, Universal Studios released *The Last Temptation of Christ.* It was called one of the most blasphemous films in movie history, making the 1973 rock opera *Jesus Christ Superstar* look like a gospel account by comparison. In *The Last Temptation of Christ,* the filmmakers managed to turn the greatest story ever told into the most blasphemous story ever dared.

If Universal had released a film ridiculing the life of Martin Luther King or the life of Moses, the outcry would have been deafening. But Hollywood, which has turned "Christian bashing" into an art form, believes it can go after Christians without major repercussions. And so Hollywood assaulted the Christian community in a way it would never have dared assault the black community, the Jewish community, and certainly not the gay community. And all because the studio executives were so sure they could get away with it.

The film is based upon the fictional account written by the Greek novelist, Nikos Kazantzakis, best known for his popular *Zorba the Greek*. But Mr. Kazantzakis went far beyond the bounds of artistic taste when he portrayed Jesus Christ as a sinner rather than as the Son of God. The novel was denounced as heresy by the Greek Orthodox Church and was removed from many library shelves.

Universal did hold a sneak preview of the movie for representatives from the National Council of Churches, Fundamentalists Anonymous, and Norman Lear's People for the American Way. You can guess what their reaction was. Nearly all of them praised the film as presenting the "human side" of Jesus.

Many thousands of people heard the "Point of View" interview I had with Don Wildmon when we discussed *The Last Temptation of Christ*. When we opened up the 1-800-number phone lines, people called to express their outrage. The feeling was that "this time we have been pushed too far." They wanted to *do* something.

Don suggested several things our listeners could do. First, he said, they could call Mr. Lew Wasserman, chairman at MCA (the company that owns Universal Pictures) and ask him why they felt it necessary to do the film.

He suggested that people distribute petitions to the

local theaters in their own communities asking theater own-
ers, out of respect to the Christians in their community, not
to show the film in their theaters.

His other suggestion was an idea that is more and
more becoming a last resort measure for getting this sort of
thing stopped. That is to boycott the offending companies.
Dr. Wildmon called for a boycott of MCA and the local theaters that chose to show the film.

Our listeners followed Dr. Wildmon's suggestion. And
they, along with other concerned Christians all over the
country, wrote letters. Did they ever write letters!
MCA/Universal received hundreds of thousands, if not millions, of letters of protest. The company received as many
as 122 thousand in a single day!

And people called. So many phone calls were placed by
people protesting the movie that the company's phone system was knocked out. One estimate said they were receiving approximately ten thousand calls a day. They would have
gotten even more, but they didn't have the capacity to receive them.

Millions of Christians signed petitions, made telephone calls, and wrote their local theaters. At first the
movie was hailed as a success. But after that first weekend
it went steadily downhill. It was a disaster for the company,
but it was a great triumph for concerned Christians.

In fact, I've never seen such a unified effort among
evangelicals, with some of the nation's top personalities
calling for a giant voice of outrage from the Christian community.

At least thirty million people throughout the United
States were involved in the protest. They either wrote letters or made telephone calls or signed petitions or marched
in protests or contacted their theaters—or they did a combination of these. And their action paid off.

After listening to and talking with Dr. Wildmon on the
program and after watching the protests, rallies, and in-

volvement of millions of people across America, I was reminded of how vital communication is. Armies have lost wars because they weren't able to communicate with their troops. And without communication within the conservative community in America, many things—such as this blasphemous movie—would never be challenged.

Some people charged that we merely gave publicity to *The Last Temptation of Christ* by bringing it to the attention of the American people. Try telling that to Lew Wasserman. And try to convince people who invested money in the film.

Oh, no. What we did was make a preemptive strike against the movie by warning people what it was all about. Without that warning, people would certainly have believed the handpicked religious leaders who so lavishly praised the film. Unsuspecting filmgoers—including many Christians— would have put millions of dollars into the hands of the very people who attacked Christ and Christianity.

Oddly enough, when Christians boycotted the movie by the millions, media coverage of the massive rejection was not to be found. Somehow the media elite didn't find our victory newsworthy.

"The Christian community won a tremendous victory," said Don Wildmon. "We joined hands and worked together, and we accomplished what appeared to be the impossible. Against tremendous odds—millions of dollars in promotion by MCA/Universal, all the support the company could rally in the Hollywood community, and hundreds of articles and broadcasts in the secular media praising the movie and criticizing those who protested it—the Christian community succeeded. It just shows what can be accomplished when we join together in a common effort."

Do Christians make a difference? You bet they do!

Letter Writing

Write letters to the editors of your local newspapers. Let them and the others readers know how you feel about the job the media are doing.

Write to your local television and radio stations, and write to the national networks (ABC, CBS, NBC).

Write to your congressional representatives. Address the letter to a specific representative, Washington, D.C. This is sufficient. You do not need a specific address.

NEWS REPORTING

The Millionaire Evening Stars

W e've always had journalists. But not until recently did we have millionaire journalists who were the subjects of movies and who became supermarket tabloid celebrities.

Without a doubt the media and their stars do virtually control the national consciousness. And they do direct the agenda for discussion and debate. The problem comes with convincing the public that this is so.

Nor is it easy to show people that even those who read newspapers and news magazines and watch the nightly news on the national networks are not fully informed on the events and issues of importance. They resent it when someone comes along and tells them they aren't getting the whole picture.

Try making statements such as these, and you will come close to being attacked. I know. I've got the mail to prove it. Some very irate people have called or written to say: "Marlin Maddoux, how dare you tell me I'm uninformed!" or "What right do you have to say I'm mistaken?"

The news media, you see, are our "window on the world." Through it we see events, opinions, and personalities displayed. If a person or an event appears on television, we automatically assume it is important. If it doesn't appear on television, we assume it isn't important—if we hear about it at all. The media, you see, tell us what to think about and, to a great extent, *how* to think.

Rarely do I watch television news without seeing evidence of how America is being manipulated, persuaded, or brainwashed into adopting new attitudes about religion, morals, sex, education, traditional values, free enterprise, Americanism, Marxism, world government, and world economics.

ADVOCACY JOURNALISM

I have seen "advocacy journalism" develop. There is a difference between a program such as "Point of View," in which we say up front that it's commentary and opinion and one that is supposed to be hard news. But our modern breed of journalists don't see that difference. They seem to think of the nightly news as their own private platforms to promote their particular views of what our society should be.

In my book *America Betrayed*, I cite the results of a survey conducted by Dr. Robert Lichter, head of the Center for Media and Public Affairs (a Washington, D.C.-based organization that provides nonbiased scientific monitoring of the news media), Elizabeth Richter, and Stanley Rothman, another respected political scholar. Their results proved that the beliefs of those who control the major national news outlets are far to the left of most Americans. Further, the results showed that the major news networks are controlled by people—some of them thinly disguised social reformers—whose worldviews run deeply counter to our Judeo-Christian moral values. This is not just my opinion. It is documented fact.[1]

Jean, from Percy, Illinois, called in to say, "There is an appalling ignorance on the part of many of these media spokespeople. They don't even have the first idea of what is typical American religious life."

I couldn't have agreed with her more.

"They use the terms fundamental, charismatic, and evangelical," she continued, "but they have no idea what those words really mean."

Brian, from Cleveland, Ohio, expressed the same idea. "One of my pet peeves with the media," he said, "is the way they describe everything from the Ayatollah to snake handlers in the South as fundamentalists."

One of the side benefits of being the host of a nation-wide talk show is that I get to visit with many of the people I admire. So I counted it a special honor to spend some time with Dr. Robert Lichter on "Point of View." I interviewed him by telephone from his office in Washington, D.C.

Here's how Dr. Lichter explained the situation: "We feel that the media has become so much a part of the political process in America, and they're out there monitoring how every group is doing. So what we're doing is watching the watchdogs. We're seeing what sources are getting quoted and what themes are coming up in the coverage and what stories are not being covered so that people won't be completely dependent on the news for their source of information."

And just who makes up this new elite group of media journalists? Dr. Lichter defined them as the people who bring us the network news—ABC, CBS, NBC, and PBS; the nationally influential newspapers such as the *New York Times, Washington Post,* and *Wall Street Journal;* and the major news magazines—*Time, Newsweek,* and *U.S. News and World Report.*

"We took a Gallup-type poll of a random sample of these journalists," Dr. Lichter told me.

One of the first things they found was that this group of elitists was very homogeneous and "tended to be politically liberal, democratic, and cosmopolitan. Most of them came from big cities in the Northeast."

Most tend to have secular backgrounds. While 90 percent of the general public say religion is important in their lives, only half the leading news executives claim any religion at all, and fewer than one in five ever attend church or synagogue.

Interesting? Here's more:

- On the abortion issue, 90 percent are pro-choice.
- On homosexuality, over 80 percent reject the notion that homosexuality is wrong.
- Forty-seven percent see nothing wrong with adultery.
- Politically, they tend to be liberal. In the 1972 Nixon sweep over McGovern, for instance, 81 percent of these journalists voted for George McGovern.
- Four out of five endorse strong affirmative action for minorities.
- A majority believes that America's use of resources is immoral. (We use too much relative to the rest of the world.) A high percentage of them agrees with the standard Soviet propaganda line that charges that the United States exploits developing countries of the world.
- Fully half believe that the very structure of American society causes alienation.
- Twenty-eight percent say our institutions need a complete overhaul from the ground up.
- Two out of five think that big corporations should be taken over and run by the state.

Now, lest you get the wrong impression, let me assure you that Dr. Lichter, Elizabeth Richter, and Dr. Rothman are not on a crusade against the press. They are merely political scientists who have taken a hard look at the media within the larger context of social and political leadership in America. The results of their work are contained in a factual, hard-hitting book entitled *The Media Elite: America's New Power Brokers*.

According to the book, the media elite not only reports the news, but its members have become brokers of enormous power in the economic, social, and political arenas. (This book is such a valuable work that we have made it required reading for everyone who goes to work in the news department of the USA Radio Network.)

The Monopoly of the Media Elite

David Brinkley made a statement that reflects the "elitist" mentality of many of those in major news networks. Speaking before a meeting of the Radio-Television News Directors Association, he stated that most Americans don't read newspapers for their news. Most watch television. "All they know about public policy," he boasted, "is what we tell them."

Unfortunately, Brinkley is right. Television news is a monopoly, not a free-enterprise system. If you don't believe that, ask Jann S. Wenner, who was formerly editor of *Look* magazine and is now publisher of *Rolling Stone*. He told professors and students at the University of Southern California School of Journalism, "We don't have a free-wheeling, competitive, diverse, unrestricted free press as contemplated by the First Amendment, but a government regulated *monopoly*. We have a Big Three in New York just as we have a Big Three in Detroit."[2]

Or ask A. Frank Reel, author of *The Networks: How They Stole the Show*—a book written about this monopoly. According to Reel, the "lords of the television business" would like us to think their industry is a "fine example of free enterprise." But,

Free enterprise in this case is a euphemism for what is the most powerful, most effective, and most impregnable monopoly in the United States: the television network monopoly. The fact that the monster has three heads—NBC, CBS, and ABC—makes television competitive only within the most limited terms. . . . Not only do the networks dictate to local stations what we will watch, they so control the production of shows that an independent producer cannot make a profit until his show has run for four or five years. And the ratings system, which determines success or failure, is simply an organ of network propaganda. Yet the networks' profits and power are so enormous that they have been able to turn government legislation to their favor.[3]

Since I realized how much the media elite controls the news through this monopoly, I told Dr. Lichter I was not at all surprised at his findings. In fact, they confirmed what I had felt all along: that the news reporting people were biased. And I knew that they held many views contrary to those of the vast majority of Americans.

"What this all spells out to me," I said, "is that these journalists are pushing for socialism."

When he answered, "Yes, only one out of three agrees that the private enterprise system is fair to workers," I could see how Mikhail Gorbachev, Fidel Castro, and Danny Ortega managed to get so much favorable publicity.

Ex-CBS Evening News anchor Walter Cronkite, perhaps the most trusted man in American media, for years projected a model of nonpartisanship. Now, however, with public pressure off, Cronkite is showing his true orientation. Addressing a dinner meeting of the liberal People for the American Way, Mr. Cronkite spoke out on what he described as "that much-abused subject, liberalism."

Not only is Mr. Cronkite a fairly far-out liberal, it turns out, but he is passionately committed to his beliefs. "I have never disguised my sentiments about politics," he insisted.

"Liberalism came out in almost every speech in one way or another on radio."

And he was a powerful force in this country. When Reed Irvine, head of Accuracy in Media, a news-monitoring organization based in Washington, D.C., appeared on "Point of View" he told us, "Cronkite probably did more than anyone else to convince the public that our situation in Vietnam was hopeless after the 1968 Tet offensive even though the enemy had suffered a crushing defeat. In 1974 he did not report demands for building up our defenses. Only stories about those who wanted to cut defense spending were considered newsworthy."[4]

He continued: "Even North Vietnam now publicly admits that the Viet Cong forces were virtually wiped out in the Tet offensive. Had Walter Cronkite not been led by his liberal bias to spread defeatism in the wake of the biggest victory of the war, the world might have been spared a great tragedy."

Mr. Irvine concluded that "Cronkite used his powerful position as a network anchorman to influence the course of events by selective reporting of the facts and insinuating his judgments into his broadcasts."[5]

With Cronkite as the standard, is it any wonder that the networks are so left of center?

In her book *Missile Envy: The Arms Race and Nuclear War*, Dr. Helen Caldicott states:

> Journalist Walter Cronkite recently told me that for years, he has been in favor of unilateral nuclear disarmament. He thinks that America should totally disarm within ten years, and some of the money saved should be used to create satellites and communications systems to educate the people of the world about how to live in peace. The money could also be used for food programs, and to help the industrial conversion process from weapons to peace.
>
> He said he favors passive resistance—that if tens of

thousands of people just sat down in front of Russian tanks, what could they do? He said we should make the arms negotiators sit at a table, and stop the clock and lock the door until they achieve appropriate arms reductions.[6]

So much for Walter Cronkite's unbiased approach to the news.

STUDENT JOURNALISTS FURTHER TO THE LEFT

I asked Dr. Lichter about claims in his book that his survey shows the new breed of journalists to be even more liberal than the ones he originally interviewed.

"We did a survey of students at the Columbia University journalism school, which is the premiere feeder from college into the major media organizations," he said. "What we found is that these young people were well to the left of their elders in the major media."

Well to the left of their elders? That's what the man said. And if you're thinking it can't get any worse, hold on. It does.

When these future journalists—the ones who will probably be filling the most strategic spots in the most powerful media outlets in the nation—were asked about social issues, Dr. Lichter found that the older journalists and the new breed are "united in their rejection of traditional morality and their support of social liberalism. They are almost equally strong supporters of environmental protection, affirmative action, women's rights, homosexual rights, and sexual freedom in general."

Evidently the new media elite have been sufficiently trained by the secular humanists in rejecting all moral absolutes, for when it comes to their attitude toward sex and sex roles, Dr. Lichter found they are "virtually unanimous in opposing both governmental and traditional restraints."

As my guest was giving us the comparison between the older journalists and the new breed coming out of the journalism schools, he said, "You wouldn't believe that the number of media elite on the side of pro-choice could go much higher than 90 percent. But in our latest surveys it goes up to 96 percent."

He had already moved on to another subject before his statement hit me. "Hold the phone!" I said. "Wait a minute! Run that back through again. Are you saying the percentage of pro-choicers has gone from *90 percent* up to *96 percent?*"

"That's right," he said. "You'd think they couldn't get much more pro-choice than 90 percent. But they now go up to 96 percent."

If you've watched the national news or listened to the radio news you know that when the major media want an "expert," they usually drag out the same old faces and voices to give us their opinions on everything from peanut farming to nuclear warfare. "Is this an accident?" I asked Dr. Lichter.

"No," he answered. "I don't think it's an accident at all. We asked the journalism students how they would rate a number of public figures, and they rated people like Ralph Nader and Gloria Steinem and Senator Edward Kennedy very highly. People like Margaret Thatcher, Ronald Reagan, and Jeane Kirkpatrick, they rated very low. These choices reflect their own belief system. Personal preferences seem to show up in the people who become 'reliable sources' for television and the newspaper, and the preference is for the liberal side."

"Any examples?" I asked.

"Look at welfare reform," he said. "This is a subject that liberals and conservatives, Democrats and Republicans, have been pushing over the years. But when we asked journalists, 'Where would you go for reliable information on welfare reform?' they picked sources, like Jesse

Jackson, who push the National Welfare Rights Organization. In practically every case, the more liberal side was treated by these journalists as the more reliable source."

Dr. Lichter found that journalists' highest ratings went to prominent liberal figures. The most popular? Liberal "consumer advocate" Ralph Nader. He is followed by the radical feminist Gloria Steinem, liberal senator Edward Kennedy, Atlanta mayor Andrew Young, and liberal economist John Kenneth Galbraith.

Another group that comes off pretty high on their popularity list are the Communist Sandinistas down in Nicaragua. In fact, the Sandinistas are viewed more positively in the survey than any of the conservative groups in America.

On the other side, these journalists just don't seem to like some people at all. Their strongest disapproval is reserved for conservative groups and individuals. While President Reagan was pulling large numbers in the popularity polls, these media elites had him at the top of their "Don't Like" chart—even before the Iran-Contra affair. Dr. Lichter found that two out of three respondents "strongly disapprove" of Reagan, compared to only one in four who feel negatively about Fidel Castro.

Not too long ago I had Brent Bozell, chairman of Media Research Center in Alexandria, Virginia, as my guest on "Point of View." He explained that his group analyzes the major printed media in order to measure long-term trends of media bias. Then, through their monthly newsletter *Media Watch,* they distribute this information around the country to show the ongoing anticonservative bias.

"Be it in economic affairs, be it in foreign affairs, be it in religious affairs," Mr. Bozell insisted, "across the board, people in the media *do not like conservatives!*"[7]

So how much unbiased reporting do we actually get? You be the judge.

"Objective journalism," observed a caller from Montana, "is a contradiction in terms."

Said Mr. Bozell, "In the media's mind's eye, any conservative in the media today is automatically categorized as being an analyst or commentator. But when you got their liberal counterparts—the Dan Rathers, the Tom Brokaws, the Bruce Mortons, the Jeff Greenfields—they're somehow objective reporters."

Today's mediacrats seem to think they run our country. They tell us what's on the national agenda, and they even tell us what to think about.

Sam Donaldson, formerly of the White House Press Corps, made a typical snide and arrogant elitist remark. "With Bush elected to the presidency," he said, "it's a good thing ABC is giving me another assignment. I would savage George Bush."[8]

That's not reporting. And someone should have told him so.

I am especially concerned about the media's glaring admiration for leftist, Marxist regimes and the favorable coverage they receive. Dr. Lichter's research shows that new journalists rank national defense below all other goals—two out of five, in fact, consider it least important of all.

"They're very hard on right-wing dictatorships," I told Dr. Lichter, "and that's as they should be. But they're so soft on left-wing totalitarian dictatorships in places such as Cuba, Nicaragua, and the Soviet Union. And what about the media's ongoing drumbeat for Mikhail Gorbachev?"

"We looked at Gorbachev's coverage compared to Ronald Reagan's during the Washington and Moscow summits," Dr. Lichter told me. "What we found was that on the TV networks Gorbachev had about a three to one ratio of good to bad press—about three times as many positive comments as negative. Reagan, on the other hand, was criticized more often than he was praised. Gorbachev clearly carved out a sphere for himself as the man of peace and the positive force for social change."

"Why?" I asked Dr. Lichter. "What's their purpose?"

"When the media see a Communist mouthing the kinds of democratic slogans they like to hear, they respond. They're not trained sovietologists, you see. They *like* to hear this kind of rhetoric from Gorbachev. He's a good story. They *hope* what he has to say is true, so they're giving him the benefit of the doubt in their coverage."

One of the questions I have—and, I'm sure, many of you as well—is this: Can a journalist separate his own prejudices and beliefs from his job of reporting the news? Is there a relationship between how these individuals view the world and how they present the world to the public? In posing this question to Dr. Lichter, I read the following quotation from his book: "Our survey found that a majority of leading journalists do see social reform as a major role of the media. . . . A majority of the journalists surveyed believed their work should be a *force for social reform.*"

Frankly, that frightens me.

It is Dr. Lichter's belief that journalism's view of itself as a major source for social reform gained strength in a period from the mid-60s to the mid-70s when journalists became so involved in major social change movements, from civil rights to the Vietnam War to Watergate. Each time they found themselves challenging authority and, ultimately, they found themselves on the winning side. In doing so, they became rich and famous and won a lot of prizes. It's hard to argue with success. Quite understandably, this produced a powerful push towards more adversarial and reform-oriented reporting.

It used to be that reporters came out of the working class and reflected working-class liberalism. Now, they're from the yuppie class and are yuppie liberals. Their sense of social mission says that now they don't want just to transmit the news to us and tell us what the powerful are doing. They want to *translate* the news and tell us what it means. They want to tell us more than the facts; they want to tell us the *truth*. That makes them a force for social change.

Media Research Center did a survey during the Republican and Democratic conventions in 1988 and came out with a clear-cut statement that there was definite bias on the part of all four networks. They had rated each network on a scale of one to ten each evening for the four nights of the conventions.

"Which were the worst?" I asked Brent Bozell. "Give us the networks in order, from the most biased down to the least."

"In the Democratic Convention, NBC, of all people, were the best. At the Republican Convention, CNN and ABC tied for that honor. For worst place, overall, without any question, making a pathetic last place showing was CBS. They were just abysmal."[9]

That didn't surprise me a bit.

YET AMERICANS BELIEVE JOURNALISTS

You want to know something amazing? In spite of an abundance of information concerning the biases of journalists, Americans still have an ongoing love affair with the media people. The Gallup organization proved this when they surveyed more than two thousand adults, asking them to rate on a scale of one to four how much they could believe each news source.

After a study of major news organizations and personalities, the report stated: "The overwhelming majority of the general public believes most of what it hears, sees or reads in the nation's press."[10]

Only two publications failed the credibility test: the *National Enquirer* and *Rolling Stone*. Major news organizations enjoyed a more favorable rating than did Congress.

Paul called from Des Moines, Iowa, to air his concern: "The media plays to the public. To some extent the public obviously likes what they see, because they tune in."

Paul is right. It is our responsibility to think for ourselves. We need to doubt the networks' evening stars. It is imperative that we analyze what we see and hear and that we be sensitive to how it affects our own beliefs.

"Just before Super Bowl Tuesday," a caller from Missouri told our listeners, "'West 57th Street,' a CBS news show, had a piece on Pat Roberston. By the time they got through with him, he looked like the most dangerous man since Ayatollah Khomeini."

It's true of every one of us: Our values and perspectives, our worldview, play an inescapable role in all our decisions. For most of us, those decisions don't influence millions of other people. It's different with journalists, however. Their control over the enormous power of modern technology, their decisions about news stories and the words they use—these *do* influence millions.

Freedom of the press is one of the most important rights we Americans have. This freedom is to be protected at all costs. We have a right to insist that those in the media tell us up front that they are out to change the world. It is their responsibility to stop masquerading as objective journalists. We need to know them for what they are: social engineers who happen to work for a newspaper, a magazine, or a television network.

CHAPTER 5

Don't Blame the Press, Blame the Dominant Culture

I f you were a journalist and someone gave you classified information about a super-secret spy satellite which, if it were blinded, would do us irreparable harm, would you publish it? When this question was posed on television to Jack Nelson, Washington bureau chief for the *Los Angeles Times,* he didn't even have to think about it. His answer? Certainly he would, and without a second thought.[1]

Jack Nelson is a true media man.

During an early morning visit I had with Dick Bott, president of Bott Broadcasting, Dick gave me an article he had seen in the April 28, 1986, issue of *Broadcasting* magazine. "It's something you must read," he told me.

It wasn't until I was alone that night that I finally had a chance to take the article out of my briefcase and give it my attention. What I had in my hands was a review of another article which had appeared in a monograph, *TV News and the Dominant Culture.*

The article addressed the debate over whether or not journalism, particularly television journalism, is colored by a liberal-left bias. "There is no doubt this is so," John Corry, television critic for the *New York Times,* was quoted as saying. But he insisted that this was not a conscious bias, nor a deliberate one. Rather than placing the fault with the journalists themselves, he laid the blame at the door of "the dominant culture," something he described as "the product of the opinions and preferences of America's artists and intellectuals."

According to Corry, it is this dominant culture which "determines the point of view; it focuses the journalist's attention. Most importantly, it supplies the moral dimensions to his thinking, allowing him to identify goodness and just causes." And that culture, says Mr. Corry, is firmly rooted in the political left. There, within closed boundaries, it grows and flourishes. Little dissent is tolerated, and very little is found. "The right wing," he says, "is regarded, without question, as the enemy."

Mr. Corry cannot imagine that any reputable television journalist would dispute these truths. "Totalitarianism is a fact." The Soviet Union is "an expansionist empire." "A democracy is a more moral form of government."

The problem, Corry says, comes when these abstractions are blurred by special people and events, such as Gorbachev and a summit conference. He says the "value system determines the point of view" and persuades the journalists to "apply a benevolent neutrality to anti-democratic, anti-Western forces." And this becomes "increasingly apparent," he adds, as the networks become "supernational organizations—roaming the world, negotiating with foreign governments, allowing anchormen and prominent correspondents to become surrogate secretaries of state."

THE DOMINANT CULTURE'S TO BLAME

I had to read the article two or three times before I began to comprehend the gravity of the author's findings. What he seemed to be saying was that, yes indeed, television journalism in American does operate with a "liberal bias." But that's just the way things are. We need to understand it and accept it.

More disturbing still are Mr. Corry's revelations that television journalism operates under a liberal bias "but not consciously or deliberately." That is one of the most serious indictments I've ever read against our media people. What I hear Mr. Corry saying is that the bias is so inbred that the media elite truly believe they are being totally objective when, in fact, because of their liberal mindset, they are not even capable of fairness and objectivity.

Then, Mr. Corry wants us to excuse them because it's not really their fault. The "dominant culture," remember, is the entity that "determines the point of view"; it is the dominant culture that "focuses the journalist's attention." Poor, helpless journalists. What can they do?

So often we read the stories of young men and women from conservative American homes, who, because they wanted their lives to count, chose journalism as their field of work. Then, off to a large secular college they went, and from there into journalism school—all at Mom and Pop's expense, of course.

After a few years of being caught up in the "dominant culture" of their respective college campuses, these young people came back home filled with liberal ideas of transforming society into the image stamped on their brains by their college professors and their newfound peer group.

According to the findings of Mr. Corry, these products of the liberal "cookie cutter" programs in our colleges and universities emerge to write, produce, and broadcast the news to us with a glaring liberal bias—and they don't even know it! If they don't know what they're doing, how can they help it?

The article also confirms what many of us have been saying for years: the liberal colleges are robbing our young people of their Christian moral value system and are inculcating them with secular humanism. Mr. Corry says it is from the "dominant culture" that these young people get their value system. He states that "it supplies the moral dimension to [the journalist's] thinking, allowing him to identify goodness and just causes."

In other words, what we get in the end is a bunch of brainwashed zealots on a crusade. Now, isn't that a comforting thought?

So that there can be no misunderstanding about where the "moral dimensions" are coming from, Mr. Corry tells us that their culture "is rooted firmly in the political left, where it finds its own closed frame of reference." Once these young people are convinced their moral values and cultural mandates are right, they will countenance no opposition. Their "dominant culture" has imparted to them their new "moral dimension," that is, their new worldview.

Our newly emerged journalist is now able to identify "goodness" and is imbued with the evangelist's zeal for "just causes" to pursue. Of course, his ideas of "goodness" and "just causes" are different from what he had when he first became absorbed in his new "dominant culture." And—guess what?—these new causes just happen to all fall into the liberal-left category.

From Conservative to Left-Liberal

"I heard so many generalizations about media people," said John, a "Point of View" listener calling from Florida. "But no one names any names or gives specifics. How are we going to find out about these people? If we don't know our enemies, how can we fight them?"

Hang on to your hat, John. You're going to get specifics right now.

In *The Media Elite*, Dr. Robert Lichter and Stanley Rothman reveal that of those people who control the major media of this nation, 68 percent come from one of three areas of our country: 40 percent come from New York, New Jersey, or Pennsylvania; 10 percent from the New England states; and 18 percent were raised in the midwestern industrial states of Illinois, Indiana, Michigan, and Ohio. In contrast, only 3 percent hail from the entire Pacific Coast, including California.[2]

Yet, in spite of these statistics, some of the most prominent of the TV evening stars hail from conservative states and from conservative families. Dan Rather and Sam Donaldson spent their early lives and college years in Texas. Roger Mudd hails from Virginia, and Diane Sawyer from Kentucky. Steve Bell and Ken Bode both came from Iowa, and Mike Wallace grew up in the Midwest. Bode attended college in South Dakota, Wallace in Michigan, and Richard Threlkeld studied in Wisconsin.

If so many of the media elite come from conservative backgrounds, then when and where and how did they decide to drop their conservative thoughts and "mature" into full-blown political, economic, and social liberals?

A few years ago I read a most enlightening article by Dinesh D'Souza, managing editor of *Policy Review*. The article, "TV News: The Politics of Social Climbing," appeared in the August 16, 1986, issue of *Human Events*, and it traces the road to liberalism that these and other prominent journalists had traveled.

Dinesh D'Souza answered many of the questions in my mind. He writes:

> No matter where he comes from . . . the aspiring TV journalist typically adopts a left-liberal world view as he picks up the tools of the trade. There is nothing conspiratorial in this. To get their stories on the air, TV journalists have to embrace the culture of network news, either consciously or unconsciously. . . . And since the culture of television journalism is liberal, it is hardly surprising that reporters get their idea of what is news—ultimately the most ideological question in journalism—from a whole range of left-liberal assumptions, inclinations and expectations.[3]

To get their stories on the air or into print, journalists have to embrace this media culture. Not too long ago a group of parents and teachers in Mobile, Alabama, brought a suit charging that the schools were teaching the religion of humanism. Many of the reporters who poured in to cover the story came down thinking the suit was brought by people who lived in trees.

But after two or three weeks into the trial, more than one reporter became thoroughly convinced that those parents and teachers were right. The man with whom I spoke—off the record—asked a reporter from one of the major magazine biggies, "If in fact you believe they're right, why don't you write the story that way?"

"I'll see what I can do," the reporter said.

A few days later she called him back and said, "I wrote the story, but the editor up above me scuttled it. I can't get it published that way."

To understand what Mr. D'Souza called "political socialization in the newsroom," we need only look at the background of controversial journalist Sam Donaldson. Donaldson spent his childhood in El Paso, Texas, then later attended New Mexico Military Institute and Texas Western College. Apparently, he supported Barry Goldwater for President in 1964.

Donaldson once told a *Playboy* magazine interviewer that when he moved to New York and Washington, his view of the world and of politics changed so radically that whenever he returned to El Paso for a visit, he got into arguments with his friends and his Baptist mother. In Donaldson's mind, rejecting his conservative upbringing was a sign that he had matured.

In his article, Mr. D'Souza observed that "from Donaldson's caricature of his origins, one gets the sense that this same trivializing instinct is what causes him to ridicule strategic defense or supply-side economics: he regards them as notions straight out of the bovine world from which he was liberated."

In the world of journalism, it is dangerous to be a conservative.

Reporters such as Sam Donaldson "operate on different frames of ideological reference than the majority of Americans." This is what Jeff Greenfield of ABC News told Mr. D'Souza when asked "why reporters, during political conventions, repeatedly referred to 'ultraconservatives' and the 'extreme right,' but never 'ultraliberals' or the 'extreme left.'" Greenfield added that Jesse Jackson is "really a Third World radical, but he was never identified in those terms during the campaigns."

The perceived bias is not limited to politics. D'Souza observed:

> One area where Greenfield finds a definite bias is in TV coverage of social issues. "The cosmopolitan nature of the network news makes it virtually impossible for the traditionalist point of view to be aired," he says. He gives the example of a Reagan proposal to inform parents when their minor children receive contraceptives. This was nastily dubbed the "squeal rule," Greenfield says. "I have a young daughter and I want to know if she is being fitted for a diaphragm. At least this should be a proper subject for a policy debate. But most TV reporters covered the controversy as though the only people who favored the so-called squeal rule were anti-sex theocrats."[4]

D'Souza then gave information about another evening star, Tom Brokaw, telling of his journey from small town boy to big league journalist and his conversion to the liberal view. In 1983 Brokaw told *Mother Jones,* an ultraliberal magazine, that after he joined NBC and moved to New York, he "absorbed a new set of principles."

Brokaw said he moved from values similar to those held by President Reagan to something far removed from that. Now he looks back on those original values as "pretty simplistic. I don't think they have much application to what's currently wrong."

Mr. D'Souza noted some of Brokaw's revealing answers to the reporter from *Mother Jones:*

> *Mother Jones* asked: What about those who say El Salvador is moving toward democracy? "They're wrong. My job is to stay calm at the center and point out why they're wrong." Abortion? "It comes down to the question of whether a woman has the right to control her body." Capital punishment? "Barbarous."[5]

The *Washington Journalism Review* described Brokaw as "socially adept," adding that he "not only says and does the right things, he knows the right people, counting many glamorous figures from the world of art, entertainment, sports and politics among his intimate friends. In California, he ran with a rich, politically liberal crowd that sought out the company of prominent journalists."[6]

Mr. D'Souza concluded that "Donaldson and Brokaw are fairly typical of network reporters, not in personal characteristics, obviously, but in the way they view their profession as somehow congruent with the liberal world view. It is very difficult for them to recognize the social and cultural forces that have shaped their work, not only their conclusions but also their assumptions."

Walter Cronkite, granddaddy of liberal television news reporters, states that reporters are "certainly liberal, and possibly left of center as well. I think most newspapermen by definition have to be liberal."[7]

It is quite apparent that the road to making a million dollars a year as a major network anchorman is by way of dropping "outmoded" conservative values and adopting the liberal view on life, morality, economics, government, and social welfare. As Mr. D'Souza states, "To get their stories on the air, TV journalists have to embrace the culture of network news, either consciously or unconsciously."[8]

The Docudrama: True or Fiction?

All the national networks have to do is skillfully use words, images, and innuendoes—and, of course, censor contrary information—and they can whip the public into a frenzy of emotion.

Take for example the furor over the CBS docudrama, "The Atlanta Child Murders." Advance news of the program caused such a public outcry that CBS was forced to run a disclaimer stating that some of the characters and events had been fictionalized. (This was not the first time CBS had been challenged on the fairness and accuracy of one of its programs, by the way.)

Abby Mann, author of the screenplay, stated publicly that the drama was "a crusade" to show that convicted murderer Wayne Williams was actually innocent. Atlanta mayor Andrew Young denounced the CBS movie as a trial by television. Said Mayor Young, "If you want to rewrite history, and you have two million dollars and four hours of television time, you can retry any case and find them either innocent or guilty."

Advocacy journalism seems to be the new law of the land. It's an entirely different way of reporting the news. Actually, it's not really reporting the news at all. It's a way of making slanted news acceptable. Advocacy journalists, you see, think they have the right—the duty, in fact—to slant the news. They think it's their job to go out and get the stories and report all of the flaws in this country and in society as a whole. They believe they are supposed to pick and choose news stories and report them in such a way that they're going to move the rest of us to action.

"They have a goal in mind," said Charles Wiley, a veteran reporter and guest on "Point of View," "and reporting the news becomes a vehicle for reaching that goal. They have a platform to work from. They like to say, 'Well, part of our job is to raise social consciousness.' Of course, that's just another way of saying they want to brainwash you into doing what they want to do.

"When you move into advocacy journalism from objective journalism, we are talking about moving from normal news coverage to propaganda much like they have in authoritarian and totalitarian countries. That's really what it's all about."

On one of his visits to "Point of View," Reed Irvine took CBS to task for leaning to the left. One of his complaints centered around Dan Rather's interview with Fidel Castro. "Rather's softness on Cuba was first documented by Accuracy in Media a decade ago," Mr. Irvine said, "and since then he has grown even softer."

Mr. Irvine faults Mr. Rather for not challenging Castro's statement that Cuba has a clean record on drugs. "A knowledgeable journalist would have pointed out that in November 1982, Fidel Castro declared that he would cooperate with the U.S. Coast Guard in blocking the drug traffic after a Miami grand jury indicted the head of the Cuban Navy and three other Castro officials and cronies on charges of drug smuggling." Both congressional hearings and U.S. court cases have documented testimony from Cuban agents that the Castro regime was, in fact, directly involved in drug smuggling operations.

Mr. Rather also failed to challenge Castro on the issue of Soviet involvement in Central America. Either Mr. Rather was just plain ignorant, or else he made no use of State and Defense Department reports on Soviet shipments of military equipment to the Sandinistas in Nicaragua or to Salvadoran guerrillas.

"Dan Rather, the most highly paid media personality in the country, has been used as a pawn in the propaganda war for control of Central America," Mr. Irvine said. "Dan rushed to Havana at the invitation of Castro, and CBS promptly put on the air Castro's assurances that the American people have nothing to fear from Soviet adventurism in Central America." Castro's message was obligingly aired at the height of the public debate over continued U.S. funding of the Nicaraguan freedom fighters.

These media elite have taken it upon themselves to decide what we should know. They consider themselves no less than the prophets and priests of information. It's their bailiwick. In their opinion, they are the guardians of the collective American mind. It's their job, they are convinced, to set the agenda for public discussion.

But conservatives are knocking on the doors of their fortress, and the media elite are sending out their dragons. We are influencing the social and political processes.

We have the facts that prove, without a doubt, that the media elite are out of step with the vast majority of the American people. Yet those elite get respect and awe far beyond what they deserve. And people who *agree* with them have the advantage of always being presented in the very best light via national radio and television.

THE "EXPERTS" ON RADIO AND TELEVISION

Have you ever wondered why people with a conservative point of view are seldom featured on the evening news? Or when they are invited to the news commentary shows, why it is always in the role of the villain?

It's simple. You don't give your philosophical enemy a platform on which to proclaim what you consider to be his nonsense. It's your duty as a respected guardian of the national consensus to censor his views out of our collective consciousness. Besides, if you give him air time, somebody might hear him and believe what he has to say.

Even when journalists do condescend to give the views of the "enemy," it is almost always with the attitude of pity for the poor foolish soul who holds to such views. Of course they usually have two or three "enlightened" liberals standing by to snuff out any points the right-winger might make with the viewing audience.

Take Gloria Steinem, for instance. Not only is Gloria a feminist radical; she is also a media celebrity, who is called upon to express her views on sexism, religion, morality, family, and government and who is treated as an enlightened "expert" on a variety of issues.

Gloria Steinem goes around the country preaching her "gospel" of sexual liberation and feminist dogma. In a speech at the University of Tennessee, she spouted her venom against traditional values by outlining her goals for what she called the "second wave" of the feminist movement. Once again she called for "secure reproductive freedom" as a basic human right. This means abortions paid for by *your* and *my* tax money. (Have you noticed how liberals always want their agenda to be paid out of the public till?)

Ms. Steinem insisted that the feminist movement should "redefine" sexuality. Here are her words: "Because we have been brought up to believe that sex outside of marriage is immoral, we perpetuate our sexual bondage." Is it any surprise that she also wants "democratic" families where children have as much say about how the family is run as their parents do? She went so far as to state in a speech in Houston, Texas, that she looked forward to the day when we can "raise our children to believe in Self, not in God."

To the media elite, an attractive face and an ability to articulate ideas is qualification enough to be an "expert." Oh, yes. One more thing. An "expert" must also have a liberal mentality.

Contrast the visibility of Gloria Steinem with that of Phyllis Schlafly. A pro-family, pro-Christian, traditional values spokesperson, she is interviewed only when the media cannot ignore her. Not only is she far more attractive and articulate than most of the radical feminists; she also makes more sense when she speaks. Yet we don't see Mrs. Schlafly on the nightly news. You see, she doesn't speak the "party line." On those rare occasions when she is grudgingly given a bit of airtime, she is always referred to as a radical right-winger.

Eleanor Smeal, past president of the National Organization for Women (NOW), has received constant media coverage. Her radical railings have been force-fed to the American Public on a regular basis. At the same time, Beverly LaHaye, president of Concerned Women for America (CWA)—an organization with twice the membership of NOW—doesn't get a tenth the publicity. Whatever little bit she does manage to win is given begrudgingly, delivered by the evening news stars with a condescending attitude and a not-quite-so-subtle tinge of sarcasm.

Or count the number of times you've seen Faye Wattleton interviewed about the abortion issue. Is any pro-Life spokesperson given the same amount of airtime? Not a chance. Few Americans even know the names of Dr. John Wilke, president of National Right to Life Committee, or Olivia Gans, director of American Victims of Abortion.

MORAL EQUIVALENCE

A singularly disturbing point is made in Corry's article, one that has to do with showing that the way in which these journalists report the news will have a definite bearing on our national defense and the future of this nation as a free republic. It is the doctrine of "moral equivalence." Moral equivalence is one of the most dangerous lies being perpetrated by the Kremlin. And now, here it is being echoed by our own good ol' media.

Simply put, moral equivalence is the suggestion that the United States and the Soviet Union just happen to be two world superpowers, which are motivated by the same moral values and which are both out to dominate the world.

They are Tweedledee and Tweedledum. What a coincidence. This just happens to be the theme that underlies the entire Soviet-Gorbachev campaign: there is no moral difference between our system and theirs.

This belief in moral equivalence is the basis for the cries against "American imperialism" among the leftists in this country. Evidently those who cry out so loudly haven't taken a good look at history. If they had, they would have discovered that America's purpose in foreign policy is to promote republican freedom. Much of our action around the world has been to defend free people against Soviet imperialism.

But for some reason, our media elite can't seem to pronounce the words "Soviet imperialism." Their vocabulary only contains "American imperialism."

And there you have it. However they start out, America's media elite end up members of the liberal-left dominant culture. That's how the system works. They fit in; they get the stories.

When Irving R. Levine of NBC News was asked why his coverage during the economic recovery stressed those who were still out of work, he readily admitted he had tried to bring deep skepticism to the president's policies. Then he added, "It's a lot easier to get a story on the air when the unemployment rate is going up."

As Levine put it, "For producers and reporters, bad news is good news."

WHAT CAN WE DO?

Lily called "Point of View" to say, "It really puts us Christians to shame that we're not responding. If we continue, we deserve what we get."

Lily, people all across America *are* responding, but it's not enough.

The disinformation campaign against Judge Robert

Bork is a clear example of how effective the Big Lie is when you have the money to buy spots on national television. This was a low point in the American political process, with the media, special interest groups, and liberal senators all in collusion in this crusade of distortions. And do you know what? The American people bought it—hook, line, and sinker.

The Loony Left was fighting with all its might to retain the insane Supreme Court decisions of the past forty years that have wreaked havoc in our society.

As William Murchison, columnist for the *Dallas Morning News,* said in his column:

> Federal jurists of the [William O.] Douglas stamp have enlarged the rights of criminals and shrunk the rights of the policeman; they have driven prayer from the classroom; they have hustled black and white children onto school busses in search of the constitutional chimera called "racial balance"; they have wrested from state lawmakers the right to declare unborn human life a social good, worthy of protection. That was the meaning of the battle against Bork— keeping things thus, insofar as possible in the Reagan era and beyond.

The American people were subjected to one of the vilest disinformation campaigns ever waged over a domestic policy issue. The liberal left, using tactics usually reserved for the KGB, attacked the character and judicial record of a judge who, in fact, had impeccable credentials.

As the result of the left's vicious attack on Judge Bork, many of us are a little wiser. Furthermore, his attackers may have overplayed their hand. Thousands of "Point of View" listeners were outraged, and they let their senators know it.

We tried to supply our listeners with important addresses and phone numbers so that they could express their opinion on the confirmation hearings. In the end, our attempts illustrated our government's hostility to a conservative viewpoint.

A lady called "Point of View" saying she had telephoned the Senate Judiciary Committee office and they were registering people's opinion on Judge Robert Bork. I asked members of our staff to call the number and verify that it was indeed a correct number and that the committee would register their opinion. Several of the staff did so with no problem.

So, I gave the number out over the air and encouraged our listeners to make a call and register *their* opinions. Well, that's when it started. As listeners to "Point of View" started calling, they were met with increasing hostility. Moreover, listeners were being told to register their opinion with *Marlin Maddoux* and were given *our* 800 number to call.

Now, this I couldn't understand at all. So I decided to place a call myself and find out why they were giving out my number (which, by the way, we have to pay for).

I dialed the Washington number and a woman answered, "Senate Judiciary Committee."

When I said, "Hello," I was immediately greeted by a terse voice that said, "If you're calling from the *Marlin Maddoux* show, we are not taking an opinion poll. Here's the number you can call to give your opinion." And she read off my own 800 number.

I asked the woman if it was standard procedure for an office of the government to refuse to register an opinion of a citizen and then to give out the number of a nongovernmental organization. Her response was that they were flooded with calls and didn't have time for all of these "interruptions." It was at this point that I introduced myself as Marlin Maddoux.

Immediately I was turned over to the Senate Judiciary staff director. She came on the line and accused me of running a "disinformation campaign" because I was telling people they could register their opinion on the confirmation of Judge Bork with the committee. "We are not taking an opinion poll!" she repeated.

This woman was downright irate. "The senate phones are jammed and we can't get our work done!" she fumed. It seems they were getting between eight hundred and nine hundred calls per hour! The taxpayers, I suppose, aren't supposed to interfere with the important work of the senate simply because they want to get involved with the workings of the government.

"That's why we decided to give out your number," the lady told me. "We wanted you to know what it was like to not be able to get *your* work done."

Well, those of you who called must have made quite an impression on Washington, D.C., because I received a call from National Public Radio (NPR). They wanted to know what I had done to cause such an uproar. Robert Siegel, with the NPR program "All Things Considered," interviewed me for about fifteen minutes, although I don't think the interview was ever aired. Mr. Siegel did comment that we must have a large listening audience because it had been a long, long time since anything like this had hit Washington.

Do you have a telephone? Then you can make your voice heard. As an individual, you can register an opinion. In mass our opinion can open the floodgates.

**Phone number for the
Capitol Switchboard:
(202) 224-3121**

CHAPTER 6

Fairy Tales About Abortion

Mother's Day. The day we honor those who rock the cradle, and as the saying goes, "control the future of our country." Mother gets breakfast in bed. Or is taken out to brunch. Or receives flowers.

Yet today picket lines and demonstrations are also standard Mother's Day activities. The holiday reminds us of those who don't want to be mothers—women who abort their babies. It's not the media's fault that this holiday has such morbid overtones, but the coverage of these rallies and pickets is their responsibility.

A friend in Chicago was watching the six o'clock, channel 7 *Eyewitness News* on May 12, the Friday before Mother's Day, as she has day after day, week after week, for the last twelve years. "My husband says it's the best news station in Chicago," she says.

The anchor person began coverage of the local Mother's Day weekend demonstrations on abortion. All of a sudden my friend thought, *Where's the other side? These people are all pro-choice.*

The accusations made by those who were being interviewed were outright lies.

One person said the leaders of the pro-life movement were middle-aged men who've never had children.

But Randall Terry's a young man, and Susan Smith of the National Right to Life Committee is a twenty-six-year-old career woman, and Olivia Gans, founder of American Victims of Abortion, is a thirty-year-old woman who had an abortion when she was twenty-two, thought my friend.

"When is channel 7 going to give a pro-life person the opportunity to refute those lies?" she wondered.

"Pro-lifers are fascists," said the next pro-choice representative.

Not me, thought my friend, *nor the people I know who are pro-life.* She thought about the small group of picketers she'd seen in downtown Elgin recently. No swastikas there. Just a cross. And her daughter's mother-in-law, a Wisconsin housewife who was the mother of four children and the grandmother of two. And the NOEL (National Organization of Episcopalians for Life) group at her Episcopal church. Middle America, all of them.

The last interviewee indicated that "gays" were a dominant part of the pro-life movement.

My friend was furious. She had taken notes and decided to write the station. But she, like thousands of others, never did. She did, however, stop watching channel 7 news.

Months later when I decided to write about this incident in this book, I asked her to follow up and get me a transcript or tape of the newscast. I wanted facts. So she called channel 7 to obtain a copy of the newscast. At first they referred her to a television monitoring group, but the group didn't keep tapes over one month. My friend tried two other monitoring groups, at the suggestion of the first. The same policy.

She called channel 7 back and explained her plight. "Could you send me a transcript?" she asked.

"That's not our policy," the newsroom receptionist said.

When my friend persisted in her request, the woman answered, "You'd have to get a court order to get a transcript from us."

So much for the public's "right to know," a first amendment right often trumpeted by the press. Apparently the public has a "right to know" about everything but media bias.

Nowhere is the skillful manipulation by the media more blatant than in their coverage of the abortion issue.

MEDIA COVERAGE OF ABORTION

During one of our staff meetings in February of 1989 we were sitting around the table in my office going over several newspaper articles concerning recent polls on the attitudes Americans hold toward abortion. The surveys clearly showed that there is a decided shift toward the pro-life position and away from wholesale slaughter of the innocents. Yet you had to dig deep to find that conclusion; it's cleverly hidden beneath a cover of half-truths and insinuations. The way the results of the surveys are being skewed is nothing short of criminal.

Let me share with you some of the things we found at that early morning staff meeting:

In February of 1989, the *Dallas Morning News* ran a story with this headline: "Most in Texas Poll Back Abortion in Most Cases." Now, the headline is a vital part of the overall story because the majority of people are headline scanners. This means most readers make a value judgment on the entire event or situation simply by what is conveyed in the headline. Approximately half the readers never get beyond the headline.

When Marvin Olasky, journalism professor at the University of Texas, was on "Point of View" to discuss his book *Prodigal Press: The Anti-Christian Bias of the American News Media,* he told us that the "headline choice is vital in newspapers, since most readers are headline scanners and the only information they will have about a particular event or situation is what is conveyed in the headline. Leads are vital because at least half the readers who start a story are likely to read no further."

If I, like so many other readers, had gone no further with this story than the headline, I would have said to myself, "Well, there's another survey that shows people are in favor of abortion. The pro-lifers are fighting a losing battle."

The first paragraph of the article continued the chronicle: "Texans overwhelmingly believe that abortion should be legal, at least under certain circumstances. . . . The survey indicated that 63 percent of those polled support the right of women to have abortions in limited circumstances, such as to save the life of the mother or in the cases of rape or incest."

Well, I would have thought to myself, *that certainly narrows it down a bit. Maybe the public is not quite as pro-abortion as I first thought. Perhaps I'd better read a little further.*

Not until the third paragraph did the writer say that "only eighteen percent of those polled feel abortion should be permitted under any circumstances."

Say, now, I thought, *if the author had been totally objective, wouldn't his headline have read, "Only 18 Percent in Texas Favor Abortion on Demand"?* The only problem is, that would have given the reader a far different impression from the one the writer wanted to convey.

Next we looked at the cover story of the April 7, 1989, weekend edition of *USA Today.* It looked like a paid advertisement for the pro-abortion factions. It even included a chart, which cited a Harris poll, entitled: "How Public Opinion of Abortion Has Changed."

However, upon closer examination, we discovered the only categories *USA Today* bothered to print were "Favor" and "Oppose." While it showed 56 percent favor and 42 percent oppose abortion, no information or indication was given on what percent of those favoring abortion favor it *only in extreme cases,* such as rape, incest, or when the life of the mother is threatened.

But I suppose *USA Today* was so busy covering the march of the pro-abortion radicals that weekend in Washington that such real and actual figures as these would have taken away from the impact of their own self-described "media blitz" of the event. Maybe they felt it was more important that they record the messages which emanated from the shrill voices of Molly Yard, Faye Wattleton, and Norma McCorvey (the Roe in Roe v. Wade, who was busy telling everybody that those pro-lifers weren't going to change *her* law) than that they cover the fact that America is changing its mind about abortion on demand.

After our staff had finished looking over these stories, someone said he had a newspaper story that a "Point of View" listener had sent in. "You should take a look at it," he suggested.

The story was clipped out of the *Boston Globe,* a newspaper recognized as decidedly liberal. So when I was handed the paper, I wasn't prepared for what I was about to read. The March 31, 1989, headline was a real shocker, not only for what it revealed, but also because for a change someone had finally printed the truth about one of these polls.

There in bold type the headline read: "Most in U.S. Favor Ban on Majority of Abortions, Poll Finds." I rubbed my eyes a couple of times and read it again. Sure enough, that's what it said. The *Boston Globe* had the courage to tell the truth to its readers!

Here's how they reported the poll's findings:

Fifty-three percent of those polled feel abortion should be legal in *certain circumstances;* 25 percent said it should not be legal *under any circumstances.* Now, get this:

that's a total of 78 percent who are against unlimited abortion on demand! Seventy-eight percent!

There's another significant finding too. Eighty-nine percent of those polled were opposed to abortion as a means of birth control. Interesting? I certainly thought so.

I looked at The *Boston Globe* story, then back at the story in the *Dallas Morning News*. "Isn't it interesting?" I asked the staff. "The results were virtually the same in all the surveys, but two newspapers seem purposely to mislead their readers. Only one is totally candid."

This kind of misrepresentation of facts and figures can be very effective in persuading intelligent people to believe something that isn't true. I would like to think that all of us are so well read, educated, and informed that we would not be swayed by such tactics, but in fact we are not. We have a difficult time trying to distinguish between "appearances" and reality. So when we pit our own common sense against this flood of misinformation coming from much of the media, a strange thing happens. We mentally surrender to what appears to be an overwhelming consensus. This happens over and over again on issue after issue. When everyone else says, "The king has clothes on," who are we to disagree?

It works like this: if I am constantly bombarded with a lie from television, radio, movies, school, and my peer group, and if fewer and fewer people agree with me that it's a lie, at some point I will begin to believe that I'm wrong and the lie is the truth.

With the overload of media messages coming at us from every direction, there's no need for a military type of government that guards us with guns and tanks because the lords who control the media have so convinced us they are right that we can no longer conceive of an idea or value that contradicts the accepted secular value and the sociopolitical order. And those who oppose it become the enemy.

If there were laws against slanting a story, a large number of journalists would go to jail for the way they cover the issue of abortion. But, alas, in this day when the Crusading Reporter can don a cape and mask and jump into a pressmobile and roar away to set aright the nefarious values and beliefs of a misguided public, about the only restraint is the collective public disgust over such shenanigans.

As I've often told "Point of View" radio listeners, when it comes to journalistic covering of abortion and other significant issues, we must be aware and watch closely. It is our responsibility to discern the real facts behind the slanted news the press often publishes.

Now let's look at abortion clinics and demonstrations from an insider's point of view.

Abortion Clinics and Demonstrations from the Insider's Viewpoint

If you want to know about abortion clinics, ask Carol Everett. She knows them inside and out. She owned and operated several. In her years with the clinics, she has seen far more than she cares to remember. "No matter how bad you think abortion is," she told the listeners of "Point of View," "it's worse. It's a thousand times more awful than anything you can possibly imagine."

In an effort to "re-sell" herself on her own abortion, Mrs. Everett went to work for a doctor who owned a clinic. Before long, it became obvious that there was a lot of money to be made. When the doctor refused to give her an equity interest in his business, she decided to open her own clinic.

"But you aren't a doctor," I said.

"You don't need to be a doctor to open an abortion clinic in the state of Texas," she told me. "It's easy to hire a doctor. He can make fifteen hundred dollars on a Saturday morning."

"Was it a 'good' business to be in?" I asked her.

"It was from a business standpoint," she said. "Abortion clinics can be very profitable business ventures. When I opened my fifth clinic, we were on track in our plan to make a million dollars per year. But from a personal standpoint, the business was disastrous. My life was miserable. I finally came to the point where I could no longer handle the deception, the suffering, and the death that are a major part of the abortion business. And so I walked out and left it all."

If Carol Everett had her way, there would be no abortion clinics. But with abortion still legal, we must do whatever we can.

That's what Randall Terry and Operation Rescue are trying to do. And again, the media are distorting the truth about their demonstrations. Randall Terry, head of Operation Rescue, told of a rescue held in San Diego, California. The police arrested everybody, charging several leaders with felonies. The police, Mr. Terry said, were absolutely brutal. "A policeman told one woman, 'I will break your arm,' and he did! He actually broke her arm!

"This is what is worrying me, Marlin," Mr. Terry said. "The police are beginning to predetermine that they will be brutal. They are putting erroneous felonies on people. But what is most scary to me is that we have the secular media standing right there watching it all happen and then refusing to report it. They are blacking out the police brutality."

"But," I answered, "I know from experience what people are going to say. They'll say, 'Our police wouldn't do what Randall Terry is accusing them of doing.' How would you answer those doubters?"

"As for the brutality in L.A. and Dallas, we have pictures. And we have people whose bones were broken who are undoubtedly going to bring lawsuits. In Pittsburgh, women were dragged by their undergarments through the jail past the male inmates. A guard told one woman, 'I just might throw you in there with them, and they'll rape you!' He threatened her with rape! That is a criminal offense.

"Now tell me, where is 60 Minutes when this type of brutality is going on? Where are the investigative reporters who should be reporting this illegal abuse?"

Television networks are not only reporting the news inaccurately, they are also creating docudramas to influence their viewing audience.

THE DOCUDRAMA

Another bit of pro-abortion propaganda fed to television viewers was an NBC movie entitled *Roe vs. Wade*. It employed the typical heavy-handed technique of using a docudrama to sway the viewers into accepting the view of the brain trust who put the show together. This one was so lopsided that even the most rabid pro-abortionist true believer should have blushed.

The script for this movie was rewritten seventeen times. Do you suppose this was because NBC was determined to get it right? Guess again. When have the major networks ever been overly concerned about telling both sides of a story in one of their docudramas? No, NBC's reason for concern was that the viewing, product-buying public is more aware of the abortion issue today than it was a few years ago, and a growing majority of them are becoming more and more outspoken about their pro-life position.

Gary Hoblit, the film's producer-director, is unhappy over this kind of pressure on his artistic freedom. It's time to "stand firm in the face of nay-sayers and know-nothings," he said. "These small groups of tightly knit, letter-writing, pontificating self-interest groups are trying to dictate what the networks are going to show to millions of people. . . ."

No, no, Mr. Hoblit, we're not saying you can't make movies like this. What we *are* saying is that if NBC chooses to show these movies, we'll take note of who the sponsors are, and we won't buy their products.

Now, that's freedom of choice!

Fake News

The television networks are playing a new and dangerous game with the direction they're taking their news reporting. Regardless of how they may choose to sell it to the American public, the bottom line is they are going to *fake* the news. Even if their cameras weren't there to catch the action when it happened, don't worry about it, they'll *stage* it for you. I read that: *Fake it! Choreograph it! Write a script and hire actors!* It's as phony as a three-dollar bill. The bottom line is that they're lying through their teeth. Just like P. T. Barnum.

So when it fits their purposes to prove a point or reinforce a prejudice, they will stage an event, complete with trained actors, to record and show to the public. Even though they may put a line at the bottom of the screen that says "simulation" most people will assume that the networks stick close to the facts in their little news parodies. This opens up a can of worms replete with possibilities for deception, misinformation, propaganda, and downright fraud. In fact, this comes at a time when the news media is steadily losing its credibility.

ABC News has already been caught with its ethics down when they "staged" a scene with someone who looked like the American diplomat Felix Bloch handing a briefcase to another "actor" who was posing as a KGB agent. The FBI had been investigating Bloch for allegedly passing top-secret documents to the KGB. ABC even did some cute things to the footage to make it appear to be taken with an actual FBI surveillance camera. It was a little grainy, with cross hairs and an electronic time code on the film, like the undercover people use. You just knew when you saw it that this was straight out of a James Bond movie.

And, for sure, they had caught the guy "red-handed." The only problem was it was a staged event. It was a piece of flim-flam.

The gaff was so great that in a subsequent broadcast, Peter Jennings apologized to the viewers. They had failed to put "simulation" at the bottom on the screen. But Jennings did not go further and apologize for the total lack of morality in staging the scene in the first place.

Fred W. Friendly, former president of CBS News, said of the ABC story, "Peter Jennings, the network anchorman, introduced the report as an ABC exclusive . . . That was followed by the superimposed label 'Exclusive.' It was exclusive, all right. These startling and dramatic pictures were a fraud; a fraud perpetrated by ABC News, using an actor who resembled Mr. Bloch. . . . Staff members were being used to create a 'docudrama' out of 'supposed evidence' that no reporter or producer at the network had any justifiable or evidentiary reason to support. . . . Even if the network truly had hard evidence from identified sources, a simulation of any wrongful act would be a scam reminiscent of the quiz-show scandals of 1959."

And then Friendly asked the question about television news that's on the minds of millions of Americans: "Is it to continue to be a serious and responsible instrument of communications, operating under thoughtful guidelines, or is it to be twisted into an electronic carnival, in which show-biz wizardry and values obscure the line between entertainment and news?"[1]

And what about the accusations in the *New York Post,* September 27, 1989, that CBS Evening News showed faked battle footage and gave false news accounts of the war in Afghanistan on at least four occasions? Citing sources in the United States, Europe, and Asia, the *Post* states, "Most of the footage was shot by cameraman Mike Hoover, the sources said, and portions of it were used in a 1984 series that was narrated by Rather himself and later won the network a coveted Dupont Silver Baton award."

It seems that some of the action footage "was entirely fake. . . . The 1984 series was just one of many stagings by Hoover, a man in his mid-forties, who acted more like a movie director than a journalist, according to sources."[2]

Bill Carter wrote in the *New York Times,* "Behind the *New York Post*'s recent charges that CBS News broadcast misrepresented films of the war in Afghanistan are larger questions about methods and ethical standards of television news and the vulnerability of news broadcasts—and news viewers—to having drama passed off as reality . . . and the questions about Mr. Hoover restaging events are surfacing at the same time that the news divisions of two networks are producing programs that *openly recreate events using actors.*"[3]

CBS has denied the allegations. But, whether CBS is guilty of fraud or not, the point is that with the trend toward "staged" news events, you can see that the potential for using the cameras to mislead, misinform, or persuade is enormous.

Reuven Frank, former president of NBC News, now with the Gannett Center for Media Studies in New York, said, "They now subscribe to the gospel of 'do anything to get an audience.' They don't even bother to make excuses for it anymore."

And commenting on the sophistication of the networks' computer graphics departments, Frank said it is possible to fabricate news footage with a computer that looks as good as, or better than, the real thing. "As graphics get more and more sophisticated, you're not going to be able to tell the difference . . . It's marvelous for drama. For news, it's lies."[4]

We are seeing a blurring of the line between fabrication and actual news. And one of the reasons this is happening is that the networks are shifting people from their entertainment divisions to their news departments. These people bring this "entertainment" mentality with them, and it influences their approach to the news. The news will soon look like "Saturday Night Live."

In a cover story in the August 7, 1989, issue of *Time* magazine, Diane Sawyer and Sam Donaldson were featured in a puff piece for their new ABC "Prime Time Live" show. In the story titled "Star Power," *Time* asked, "Diane Sawyer, with a new prime-time show and a $1.6 million contract, is hot. But are the celebrity anchors like her upstaging the news?"

They described her as "the rich, honeyed voice; husky and authoritative, but free of the severe tone affected by some females in TV news. . . . Diane Sawyer doesn't just deliver the news; she performs it." Then the author made a statement that shouldn't be overlooked. He said, "Sawyer, more than any of her colleagues, embodies all the contradictions of TV news: that uneasy mix of journalism and show business, reporting and acting, substance and style."[5]

Who can resist the siren song of the beautiful people, beckoning us to follow them? Who wants to be "out of step" with the "in" crowd? Knowing the way human beings respond, the Pied Pipers of glamor TV play their flutes, and the hypnotized masses dance merrily after them.

Tom Shales, columnist for the *Washington Post,* said, "Important old distinctions are evaporating or being declared irrelevant. The costs of producing prime-time entertainment in Hollywood have escalated so radically that networks want to develop their own prime-time news shows, much cheaper to produce, as a viable economic alternative. If they make the news programming conform to the contours of entertainment programming, as it appears they intend to do, then television will end up even deeper down the white rabbit's hole than it already is. . . ."[6]

Kari Granville wrote in the *Los Angeles Times* that the new boom in news-based programs is "an expression of the new ethic operating in network TV: Even news, given looser standards and the right packaging, can score in the ratings."[7]

She states that, until recently, such reenactments were banned by the networks as not "meeting standards of accuracy."[8]

In making the news "more palatable" to viewers, Sid Feders, executive producer of "Yesterday, Today & Tomorrow," said, "It's a little dazzling. People like it. They know they are being entertained."[9]

Entertained? I think it's a little more serious than *entertainment.* The potential for harm is frightening. For example, can you imagine how they would "reenact" a peaceful sit-in at an abortion clinic? Of course, they would choose actors who would portray the pro-lifers as mean-spirited, unbalanced, rank radicals with no redeeming qualities.

Just consider how far this can go with 96 percent of the media elitists coming down on the pro-abortion side. Do you think for a moment that they will be "balanced" in their story? Of course not! How can they be balanced? They will show the pro-lifers as "bozos, clowns, idiots," and "dangerous" because that's the way they honestly see them through their liberal-tinted glasses. Their worldview is the filter through which all events and persons are seen. Their worldview has predetermined how they will portray the right-to-life movement. So they run a line at the bottom of your TV screen that says "simulation." Big deal! The damage is done. Most viewers would think they were watching the real thing.

On the other hand, the screaming director of the abortion clinic will be shown to be the "hero." Remember how they portrayed Norma McCorvey and Sarah Weddington in the pro-abortion movie "Roe vs. Wade." You see, you don't have to lie as long as you can cast the characters that represent your side as warm, loving, brave, and caring and characters on the other side as evil, misinformed, misguided zealots. Neat trick if you can get away with it. And the media are getting away with it.

Professional journalism has to return to a fair and balanced reporting of the news if America is to survive as a free nation. And it has to begin in the journalism schools. Too long they have produced zealots who are "cleverly disguised social engineers" posing as journalists. And the news industry as a whole should denounce these *avant garde,* show biz programs, docudramas and staged events that are being passed off as news.

But, to be honest with you, I don't think they will do it. I think this is the direction the network news is headed. And I would suggest that you tighten your seat belts; the ride into the future is going to be rough. For Christians and conservatives, that is. On the other hand, the leftists will come off looking like Wonder Woman and Captain America.

CHAPTER 7

Fairy Tales About Woodstock, AIDS, and School Textbooks

Remember Woodstock? In August of 1989, the twentieth anniversary of the event, everyone seemed to. On the August 4, 1989, edition of ABC's news program, "20/20," Hugh Downs told us that reporter Lynn Sherr "has gone to find those now-grown children of Aquarius."

We were treated to such memories as "One of the best parties I ever went to," "Great music," "There was a lot of kindness and a lot of helping people," and "It was a lot of love expressed."

"The anthems to peace that so captivated a generation were in stark contrast to the violence of the decade," Ms. Sherr reported. "But for three days in upstate New York, there was no violence. Those who were there say it's because the half a million kids policed themselves."

Doesn't it sound wonderful? All that peace and kindness and helpfulness and love? Funny thing is, that isn't exactly what I remember from August of 1969. What I remember centered mostly around drugs.

"In retrospect," Ms. Sherr continued, "all the dope reflected a more innocent attitude toward drugs."

I was still pondering the fond memories of Woodstock coming at me from everywhere when I was shown a letter to the editor printed in the *Santa Barbara News Press* on

August 28, 1989. It was written by a man named David Heidelberger.

"It's time for someone to point out that Woodstock was a disastrous failure as an enterprise, was mediocre as an entertainment event, and is not remembered affectionately by every citizen in this country," Mr. Heidelberger wrote.

"This one failed, ironically, because the love children tore down the fences and stole the festival from the organizers. Wonderful group.

"The absence of law enforcement was an imitation, a parody of peace, and self-indulgence masqueraded as a pathetic caricature of love. There was love, if by that misuse of the word you wish to mean there was little hatred. But what's to love or hate when your brain is so scattered by drugs that your emotions become little more than debris to be bulldozed about by the mob?

". . . Remembering Woodstock has been a resounding success. Unfortunately, for all the wrong reasons."

Now, that sounds more like my recollections. So who's right, Mr. Heidelberger and me, or "20/20" and just about every other journalist revisiting the event? To find out I went to the library and back to 1969. Here's what I found:

Love? "Fully half the immense crowd jammed into the amphitheater had not paid the $7 ticket."[1]

Peace? "In explaining the few arrests on the fairgrounds, one policeman said there were not enough jails in the country to hold those breaking the law."[2]

And what about that "more innocent attitude toward drugs"? "'How many of the crowd are smoking grass?' scores of youths were asked in a spot check of the situation. The almost unanimous response was: Ninety-nine percent."[3]

"'Grass' was not the only thing used here. There was also—unfortunately for scores of youngsters, and deadly for at least one so far—LSD . . . ; amphetamines . . . ; and assorted other drugs that are 'dropped' or 'popped' or 'toked' or sniffed or swallowed."[4]

Barry Farrell, writing for *Life* magazine, wrote: "The press and even the police seem content to write it off as a victory for peace and love, which, in a way, it was. But I would have thought that the significance of a half-million young Americans spontaneously creating a society based on drugs would have caused some slight concern."[5]

I would have thought so, too.

In a prophetic moment Farrell summed up his piece this way: "It was a groovy show, all right, but I fear it will grow groovier in memory, when this market in our madness leads on to shows we'd rather not see."[6]

I wonder if Barry Farrell saw the August 4, 1989, edition of "20/20."

Do you see the pattern here? It's not truth you're seeing on television. Nor is it straight facts you're reading in those daily newspapers and news magazines. What you *are* seeing and reading is what the media elite *want* you to see and read.

AMBUSHING THE AIDS EPIDEMIC

Not only do the media present their "facts" in such a way as to keep the news in line with their own agenda, but they also fall prey to the pressures of special interest groups.

Perhaps this is the reason AIDS seems to be the only disease in human history with real political clout. While our medical professionals continue to mislead us, our national media men and women—the very ones who should be sounding the alarm—are pulling off the greatest cover-up in history. It's bigger than Watergate. In the national media we see no more than a hint that homosexual practices are the major cause of the spread of AIDS, and that, in the interest of survival, such practices should be outlawed.

And yet how can we expect the truth from our media when so many of our newspeople believe there is nothing wrong with homosexuality?

The cover story of the January 12, 1987, *U.S. News and World Report,* was entitled: "AIDS: At the Dawn of Fear." In one of the boldest statements made about the disaster the article said, "It [AIDS] is today a crisis for the U.S. more deadly than many wars of modern times. In just four more years, the disease will have killed more Americans than the Vietnam and Korean Wars combined."

The statistics given in the article should alarm any thinking person into realizing that we are now facing one of the most ominous threats of modern time. It is even greater than the atomic bomb:

> As of the end of 1986, more than 29,000 Americans had contracted AIDS. By 1991, according to the most conservative estimates, 270,000 people will have been stricken, 179,000 will have died—and new cases involving heterosexuals will have multiplied ten-fold to 23,000. Almost 4,000 babies will have contracted the virus while in their mother's wombs. The Center for Disease Control estimates that 1.5 million Americans now carry the virus but display no symptoms. Others think that number may be as high as 4 million. Conceivably, all of these people could progress to the incurable disease; certainly a fourth to a half will. With no effective cure in sight, all those who fall sick are doomed.

The article then posed the question, "Why, then, have public-health officials soft-pedaled their estimates?" Mathilde Krim, associate research scientist at St. Lukes-Roosevelt Hospital Center and co-chairperson of the American Foundation for AIDS Research, is quoted as saying: "As well intentioned as health officials may be, they are lulling people into complacency. Conservative projections will cost the lives of thousands of people."

A most unbelievable social phenomenon surrounds the AIDS epidemic. What we have is a disease with the potential for wiping out the human race. It was introduced into the United States by homosexuals through their dubious "lovemaking," then spread to prostitutes and to their "tricks," to intravenous drug users, to the blood supply, to heterosexuals. Now it poses a threat to every person in America and, ultimately, to every man, woman, and child in the entire world.

Yet, according to our media, no blame is to be laid at the feet of the homosexuals. And certainly nothing is to be said about their sexual acts or their incredible promiscuity. That would be "judgmental." After all, this is the day of "sexual liberation," and what a person does in private is his or her own business. That's what they say. And if any of us so much as hints that there should be an abandonment of homosexual practices or that homosexuality should be stigmatized in any way, that person is immediately branded a Nazi—or worse.

While this incurable disease continues to be spread among us, the national media cover-up persists. Awards are given for "sensitive" films glorifying the "gay" lifestyle. Television programs are shown to the American public portraying the "gays" as the heroes and the "straights" as the villains. And we are told that if we have a "problem" with the gay lifestyle, then we are the ones who need psychiatric care because we are suffering from "homophobia."

The incredible stranglehold that the homosexual pressure groups have on the entertainment industry was illustrated by a "Schoolbreak Special" that was aired nationwide May 13, 1987, entitled "What If I'm Gay?" The program, clearly directed at young people, told viewers that homosexuality is just a different lifestyle that can be "very dignified and fulfilling."

According to an article in *Human Events* (May 30, 1987), Accuracy in Media wrote CBS President Tisch complaining about this pro-homosexual program. A month later

George Dessart, CBS vice president for program practices, responded by stating that the program "provided a valuable and informed service, of which we can be justly proud, to its intended audience."

The high school student in the program was wrestling with homosexual feelings. Never once was he told he could reject them. While the rest of the world is concerned about the spread of AIDS through homosexual practices, the student was told that he had nothing to worry about if he got certain information and took precautions. Of course, there was not even a suggestion that the homosexual lifestyle is mainly responsible for the spread of AIDS. Basically, the high school student in the program was given one piece of advice: join the gay rights movement.

No, the media are not the solution. They are part of the problem.

Cal Thomas, a nationally syndicated columnist who writes for the *Los Angeles Times* syndicate, is one of only a handful of journalists who has had the courage to "tell it like it is" on the issue of homosexual practices and their link to the spread of AIDS. He wrote:

> The one thing the media does not want to say, because it fears being labeled 'judgmental,' is that the AIDS epidemic was launched by the promiscuous behavior of a subculture of homosexual and bisexual men who engaged in frequent and indiscriminate anal intercourse with other men. If they would stop that form of intercourse, or at the very least take precautions, they would not get AIDS.
>
> Most politicians fear the clout of homosexuals and are afraid to tell them to stop doing what causes the disease. . . .[7]

Fortunately, there are some other columnists—although still all too few—who are beginning to tell the truth about the causes of the spread of AIDS. In his column of June 6, 1987, George Will wrote:

Earnestly, and with applause from journalists, politicians are saying about AIDS: candor, regardless of the cost. But truths are being blurred because they inconvenience a political agenda and shock sensibilities. The agenda is to avoid giving offense to certain factions and to avoid something more terrifying than AIDS—the accusation of "discrimination."[8]

Too bad George Will and other columnists and media people didn't hear Dr. Paul Cameron on "Point of View" in 1983. These are the very things he was telling the American people back then. Instead, he was vilified and threatened with bodily harm because he dared pull back the curtain and expose what goes on in secret between homosexuals. He called homosexual activity what it is: the breeding ground for the AIDS virus.

The simple fact is that AIDS is a threat to every one of us, and sane, compassionate measures must be taken. Our national media, for the sake of us all, must become responsible in their reporting of the facts. They must cease their promotion of a lifestyle that is turning thousands of people into "the walking dead."

The party's over. And we had better face it.

THE TEXTBOOK NEWS FROM TENNESSEE SCHOOLS

By now most of you are probably acquainted with those "fundamentalist" parents down in Tennessee who objected to their children's reading "harmless" books, ones read by practically every other school child in America. The only possible explanation for those people's behavior is that they are throwbacks from the Dark Ages. At least that's likely the conclusion you have come to if you believe what you read in the evening paper or saw on television network news.

On the other hand, could it be that our liberal media did yet another con job on the American public? Is it possible that what you saw and read wasn't exactly as it happened? Well, let's take a look at the facts.

In September 1983, several concerned parents in Hawkins County, Tennessee, voiced some objections—on religious grounds—to the contents of the readers being used in their children's classrooms. The parents requested that the school district let their children read alternative readers, ones already being used in other Tennessee school districts.

At first the school went along with the request, but then it reversed itself and ordered the children to read the controversial books. About a dozen students who wouldn't comply with the directive were either suspended or expelled. When U.S. District Judge Thomas Hull ruled that the Hawkins County school board must accommodate the families' right to a free public education without violating their first amendment rights to religious freedom, the press began to cry "censorship." A replay of the Scopes trial, they called it.

Kristi Unbreit, a reporter for the Associated Press, started her article off by saying:

> Fundamentalist Christian children have the right not to read schoolbooks that their parents find offensive. . . . The parents said the books contain references to witchcraft, exotic religions, one-world government, and relative ethics. *The Diary of Anne Frank* was objected to because its young Jewish author, who died in a Nazi concentration camp, calls for toleration of all religions. *The Wizard of Oz* was deemed objectionable by the parents because it tells children that traits such as courage, intelligence, and compassion are personally developed rather than God-given, and the story depicts a witch as good.[9]

Well, all across America, people read this report and

others similar to it, and they seethed with rage at these "bigoted, fundamentalist Christian freaks." And no wonder. If the charges were true, I would be angered too. But they weren't. The news reports of that event are classic examples of reporters' bias in slanting the truth. The saddest thing about it is that most Americans never knew the truth.

The fact of the matter is that—contrary to what you read in the newspaper—these parents *didn't* object to the books stated. And the press cannot plead ignorance of the facts, either, because they were confronted with their inaccuracies. The bottom line is that they quite simply chose to ignore the truth.

According to a column by Kerby Anderson in the *Dallas Morning News* (November 3, 1986), Al Dale of ABC interviewed Vicky Frost and attorney Michael Ferris three days before the trial began in July. Mr. Dale asked them why they objected to "The Three Little Pigs" and "Goldilocks and the Three Bears." They informed him that neither they nor any of the plaintiffs in the case objected to either of these stories. In fact, these stories were in the first-grade reader the plaintiffs agreed was a good textbook.

Their lawsuit was filed only on the textbook readers used in the second grade and up. Clearly Mr. Dale's charge was wrong. Yet even though he was apprised of the facts, the end result was an erroneous report. Here's how Mr. Anderson told it:

> After the decision, attorney Michael Ferris held a press conference. During the press conference, he was asked why the plaintiffs objected to *The Wizard of Oz* and *The Diary of Anne Frank*. He corrected the reporter's accusations by noting that the plaintiffs did not object to these works, but rather to the treatment of the stories and the teachers' guide which selected particular portions for emphasis.

But even though this clarification was made at the press conference and emphasized in an earlier press release, Bob Abernathy of NBC (who asked many of these questions at the press conference) began his news story that night with a lead-in statement that listed *The Wizard of Oz* and *The Diary of Anne Frank* as books the plaintiffs objected to.

It seems the real fairy tale was not "The Three Little Pigs." It was the news reporters' stories.

The Tennessee textbook suit was brought by concerned parents because they objected to a particular series of books—the 1983 editions of the Holt, Rinehart and Winston readers. It is interesting to note that an earlier edition of these reading textbooks had been rejected for use in Texas several years before. Mel Gabler, conservative textbook researcher, told the "Point of View" audience that they had "thoroughly reviewed the Holt, Rinehart and Winston series in 1980 and found them to have a consistent theme that was antibiblical and antiChristian."

When Judge Thomas Hull heard the full story during the trial, he was convinced that the readers did, indeed, push a clear ideological agenda just as the parents had charged. He wrote, "There is no question that the reading texts teach more than just how to read."

It was revealed that these basic reading textbooks from Holt, Rinehart and Winston—designed for grades two through eight—include about thirty-five stories showing children lying or rebelling against authority with no negative consequences. They also heavily promote pacifism without showing the other side.

But it was in the area of the Christian faith that the series was most objectionable. It clearly distorted—or excluded—both Christianity and Judaism. The authorship of the gospels is erroneously attributed to "Jewish scribes." One of the stories says King Solomon received his wisdom by "talking to the animals." And yet Buddhism, American Indian religions, and various other faiths were treated favorably.

One of the recurrent themes in the reading series is feminism. One seventh-grade text blatantly declared to the young readers that "the history of mankind is the history of repeated injuries and usurpation on the part of man toward woman, having in direct object the establishment of an absolute tyranny over her."

Of course, when a radical feminist news reporter reads this in a textbook, she doesn't see anything wrong with it. To the contrary, she sees it as a way to bring about the kind of sexless society championed by many radical feminists. Anyone who believes such a person would write a fair and objective report on the Tennessee textbook trial, must have been living in a hollow tree for the past twenty years.

Since it was not *The Wizard of Oz* per se that the parents were objecting to, what was it about the book that caused them concern? It was the overall occultic themes, particularly in the teachers' manuals. As Mr. Gabler said, "The stories emphasize material on the occult, and even ask the children to write magical chants and play the role of a fortune-teller."

The main point at issue in the trial concerned the parents' free exercise of religion and, most importantly, parental rights and responsibilities concerning the education of their young children. So, when Judge Hull ruled that the Hawkins County School District could accommodate the religious beliefs of the families by allowing them to opt out of the reading class and learn reading at home, under the requirements of the Tennessee home schooling law, he was reaffirming the first amendment rights of the parents.

Had they chosen to report it in a fair and balanced manner, the national media could have done our country a great service. But they didn't. Instead, their "dominant culture" had so molded their thought processes that they could not conceive of this lawsuit having any merit whatsoever. The media did such a poor job on the Tennessee case that the truth never reached you and me, the American public. Even worse, the news was twisted to cause animosity toward Christians and their values.

ANIMOSITY TOWARD CHRISTIAN VALUES

Not only is it wrong to manipulate people this way; it is downright dangerous. It's causing a rise in animosity toward anyone who holds to Christian moral views. What we are witnessing is a rising tide of "intolerance of intolerance." The message is, if you hold to Christian moral views, you are being "intolerant" of other people's views, and that is not going to be "tolerated."

Let me give you an example. I was watching the Phil Donahue program one morning when he was interviewing some young men who were trying to provide a sort of "halfway house" for people who wanted to "escape" from Christianity. In reference to Christians, Mr. Donahue used the term "dangerous" five times during the one-hour show. He characterized it as "dangerous" for society to allow parents to "indoctrinate" their children with fundamental Christian beliefs.

Lifting his voice, Mr. Donahue shouted out to the audience, "How long are we going to allow such 'dangerous' practices to continue?"

I'll tell you, you should have seen the audience's anger rise against those "dangerous" Christian parents who dared warp the minds of their innocent children with "Christian indoctrination!"

The media is being used to create an atmosphere of hostility toward Christians and Christianity. The "New Morality" being promoted on national television advances the belief that there are no "right" answers and no "wrong" answers to moral questions. There are only answers that are right or wrong for you. And if you insist that there *are* right answers—such as biblical morality—you are told you are "intolerant" of others' views and that you are trying to "impose" your narrow-minded system of morality on them. And in our pluralistic society, they say, that is not acceptable.

A clear case in point is the issue of homosexuality. Christians believe that the Bible teaches homosexuality is a sin and an unspeakable perversion. But the new view being promoted is that it is neither a sin nor a perversion. Psychiatrists now say it is not even a sickness. It's just an "alternative lifestyle."

The liberal and "enlightened" view is that if you want to be heterosexual, then hooray for you. Homosexuals won't condemn you. They will "affirm" you in your lifestyle. But they go on to say that you in like manner are to accept, affirm, and approve of their choice of a homosexual lifestyle as being just a matter of "sexual orientation."

The clear message coming to us through the media is this: "If you don't behave in this way, we are going to call you bigoted and intolerant, and we are going to do it publicly."

Unfortunately, while the media have been preoccupied with attacking religion in general and Christianity in particular, they have totally missed one of this century's greatest stories—the worldwide explosive growth of the Christian evangelical movement.

MEDIA BLINDNESS TO RELIGION

The singular blindness of the American press concerning the vibrant Christian movement in America is one of the twentieth century's monumental tragedies. Not only is it sad for the press, but it has caused great harm to the vast majority of Americans who still hold to traditional religious and moral values.

The press has consistently covered Christian events and personalities with a certain disdainful amusement. At the same time they have continued to sound "alarm" bells warning that if this movement continues to grow, somehow it will constitute a real threat to our freedom.

The fact the press always seems to ignore is that, according to a 1985 Gallup poll, in less than a decade evangelicals grew in number from forty million to some ninety million. They have also disregarded the evidence that indicates that 90 percent of Americans believe in a personal God, that 40 percent or more attend church weekly, and that by every measurement applied, America grew more religious in the 1980s than it had been for decades. Rather interesting statistics to overlook, don't you think?

David Aikman, a native of Great Britain and correspondent for *Time* magazine, addressed this issue of the press evading the growth of the evangelical church when he wrote:

> All of these developments were barely noticed by the American media. Overseas, of course, the rapid growth of Christian churches in the Third World escaped notice altogether on the part of the stars of investigative journalism. . . . The failure to observe at all, not to mention analyze and explain, the rise of evangelical Christianity in the U.S. over a period of two decades must constitute one of the great modern blind spots of the American journalistic mind. . . .
>
> This singular media blindness has all sorts of unpleasant consequences, and not just among American evangelical Christians who have had to endure the many prejudices—born of ignorance—that swoop around the public market place. . . . In fact, U.S. news organizations have at times displayed open hostility towards any Christian organization

with a high profile and explicit evangelical positions, tarring much of Christendom with the opprobrium earned by only a small part of it.[10]

Some evangelicals can personally testify to the media's ignorance of the evangelical movement.

A Personal Example

Dr. Larry Poland—president of Mastermedia International, Inc., a ministry to leaders in film and television—told me of an incident involving Mr. Tim Penland, which illustrates the press's ignorance of the evangelical movement.

"One of the major producers of Broadway shows invited Mr. Penland to attend a meeting to see the possibilities of promoting a religiously oriented Broadway show," Dr. Larry Poland told me, "and I went along. While Mr. Penland was hung up in traffic, the producers drilled me on what Mr. Penland did and who the market was out there. They didn't have the foggiest notion that there are 82.5 million people in America who profess to be born-again. They didn't understand our lingo. They hadn't the slightest idea what we believe or what our values are.

"I think that's part of the great chasm of misunderstanding that exists between the media and the Christians."

"We prepared a six-page marketing paper called 'The Christian Marketplace,'" Dr. Poland continued. "In it we defined statistics on us—1,300 radio stations, 350 television stations, and so forth. I have given that paper to heads of networks and production companies. When they read it, they can't believe there's so much power and numerical strength behind people who claim the name of Christ across America."

I could understand what Dr. Poland was saying because I'd had a similar experience. In 1980 when I was doing remote coverage of the National Affairs Briefing in

Dallas where presidential candidate Ronald Reagan spoke, the head of the NBC television crew sat at my radio table and questioned me about who these people were. He had never heard of evangelical Christians. He didn't know we existed.

You might use the new Gallup polls and Dr. Poland's marketing power to convince your local media to give more extensive coverage to evangelical issues and spokespersons. You might also give your local press some facts from a recent study on religion and reporting and readership in the public press by Judy Weidman, editor/director of Religious News Service, and Stewart Hoover of Temple University. This study proves, for instance, that Christians are a greater part of the newspaper audience than press executives have believed.

A Study of Religion and Reporting

The authors interviewed religion writers and editors at eight newspapers and members of six church congregations in the Philadelphia area. In conjunction with this, George Gallup conducted two national surveys of eleven hundred people. Gallup found:

- The vast majority of newspaper readers consider themselves to be religious people.
- Fully half say that religion is "very important" in their lives. Eighty-one percent altogether say that religion is at least "fairly important."
- Of those surveyed, 71 percent report being daily readers of newspapers. Of those readers, again 81 percent say religion is at least "fairly important" in their lives.
- More than half of the overall sample feel it is at least fairly important for newspapers to cover religion as well as other kinds of news. About 80 percent of those for whom religion coverage is important are daily readers.

The authors then contrasted this study with their interviews with the religion writers and editors. When these newspeople were given nine "non-news" categories and asked which is "very important" to cover, only 23 percent said religion. Education ranked first at 44 percent, followed by health (41 percent) and then business (23 percent). Religion was fourth, followed by sports (21 percent).

The authors used these same categories to ask the members of the six Philadelphia area congregations how they would rate the coverage in the newspapers they read regularly.

"In terms of satisfaction with coverage," said Dr. Hoover, "the highest percentage report coverage of sports being 'excellent' (36 percent)." Only 12 percent judged the religion coverage as excellent.[11]

No wonder, since the press either ignores the evangelical movement or twists the facts to make evangelicals look like bigots or religious fanatics.

If the media blitz against Christians continues, a further step will be a rising rage of hatred against all Christians who believe, practice, and seek to share their faith. This will be followed by more severe social ostracism, then by more and more restrictive laws against our religious liberties.

Yes, they are doing it to us. And this is where it's leading us.

CHAPTER 8

Retelling the News from Nicaragua

The media can control your thoughts. They can make you like what they want you to like; they can make you hate what they want you to hate; they can cause you to change what they want you to change. They do it by skillful manipulation of pictures and of the printed word. They do it through newspapers and magazines, on television and in the movies.

I have no problem with news reporting—even when the news isn't what I want it to be—*if* the reporting is fair and balanced. You see, I truly believe that when the American people are given proper, balanced, and fair information, they are bright enough to make intelligent decisions for themselves.

The problem is that some media outlets are so blatant with their liberal bias that they no longer even seem to try to disguise it. National Public Radio (NPR) fits into this category.

In fact, on one of my broadcasts I gave the "Point of View" Fairy Tale Award to NPR for a story they did on Nicaragua. (Some people have called NPR "The Voice of Managua.")

I listened to the reporter, speaking in his most serious tones, as he painted the Marxist dictatorship as the "wave of the future for mankind." They were, according to the reporter, compassionate agrarian reformers. And the good old U.S. of A.? Why, we were the *real* evil empire, desperately trying to subject the poor Nicaraguans to slavery. It was the "sainted Sandinistas" who were the "true saviors."

Then, in keeping with "objective" reporting, they "interviewed" several farmers—picked at random, I'm sure—who live on farm communes. One by one the farmers expressed how great it was to work for the good of everyone, not just themselves. "Why," one of the farmers gushed, "when one of us has to go away, we know that the other farmers will unselfishly step in and do our work."

After listening to this drivel promoting the Communist paradise in such glowing terms, I was tempted to pack up and move our headquarters to Managua and broadcast "Point of View" from there (tongue firmly in cheek, you understand).

The report was a complete fairy tale. It was a hoax. A piece of misinformation. It was slanted. One-sided. A "puff" piece for a totalitarian bunch of hoods. Yet it was broadcast to the American people on National Public Radio—and your tax money helped to make it all possible!

How do the media do it to us? Here's one way. With your tax dollars.

And while we're on the subject of National Public Radio, I'd like to tell you about a very interesting article I came across while I was scanning through the February 28, 1987, issue of *Human Events.* The article was headlined, "Communist Reader Praises 'Very Liberal' NPR." According to the article, "National Public Radio has received some lavish praise, but it is doubtful that the folks at NPR will welcome the plaudits." It then printed a most favorable letter which had appeared in The U.S. Communist newspaper, *People's Daily World,* on January 21, 1987:

Readers of *People's Daily World* who are interested in

clear, in-depth coverage of the news from a very liberal viewpoint should try listening to National Public Radio. The "All Things Considered" program carried on NPR does stories on a variety of topics and also goes fairly deep into detail about events in socialist countries. It also includes a lot of material on Nicaragua.

"All Things Considered" is only one of their great programs. As a matter of courtesy, NPR does, at times, allow conservatives to express their opinions, but the NPR stations are listener-supported, and that keeps them relatively free of the capitalist yoke.

The letter that *Human Events* quoted is a devastating indictment on a radio network that is supposed to be a fair and objective news source. But even a cursory monitoring of its programs will quickly reveal its bias.

MEDIA BIAS

Have you ever noticed that many media people take black and white facts and numbers and make them appear to say just the opposite of what they really say? And they do it in such a way that the public never catches on. Personally, I find that exceedingly distasteful. It's yellow journalism at its worst, yet it's being done every single day.

Once again let me caution you: The liberal press in America—including major networks and many of our nation's largest newspapers and magazines—are *not* giving you factual, unbiased stories. Often, they are not even giving you the absolute truth. What they are giving you is their side of the story. Sometimes that means they're holding back certain elements which would give you a totally different impression from the one you get. With the skillful placing of a few words or figures or illustrations, the tone of the story can be completely changed. It's not that they lie exactly; they just mislead.

For most of us, the media is our main source of

information—and they know it. We have seen proof that the media elite use their power as guardians over what we should know to bring about their own desired results.

Central America is a classic example of this. President Reagan was elected largely because he promoted a strong national defense and because he promised aid to those movements around the world that would rise up and cast off their Communist oppressors. He was voicing the American people's desire to see freedom prevail, to see others allowed to live their lives in peace rather than in fear.

Yet, for some strange reason, the media elitists seem to continue to think that Communist dictatorships are simply "progressive" movements that should be left alone. Even our own state department's policy has been "once Communist, always Communist." And the media marches lock-step in line with this thinking.

THE NEWS FROM NICARAGUA

"The Iran-Contra coverage," said Reed Irvine, "has eroded the public's confidence in the media. Some of our best known newsmen led young Americans to believe the American press has a political orientation in tune with their own sentiments."[1]

The Iran-Contra affair should never have happened. It was a tragic mistake. And part of the blame falls squarely on the shoulders of the press. But don't hold your breath waiting for Dan Rather, Sam Donaldson, or Tom Brokaw to say on the evening news, "Gosh, folks, you know, if we had just given you the truth about Nicaragua, things would have turned out a lot differently. You would have put pressure on Congress and they would have given the Freedom Fighters the aid they needed and we wouldn't have another Soviet base at our back door. But we know what's best for you—and for the world, for that matter—so we gave you the information we wanted you to have.

"Now that the Freedom Fighters have bled to death in the jungles, and Daniel Ortega and his Communist dwarfs have consolidated their power and are continuing their 'war without borders,' we can tell you that, once again, we have proven that we in the fourth estate are really the ones who are running this country. But, of course, since you don't elect us, you can't vote us out."

I personally heard President Reagan express his frustration over this very issue when I met with him in the White House. There were about fifteen of us seated around a large table in the conference room a few doors down from the Oval Office. Pat Buchanan, communications director for the White House, told us that he knew of our support for the president's policy in Central America. He also said if we worked hard we might still be able to win support for the Freedom Fighters and so thwart the plans of Gorbachev, Castro, Ortega, and the other Communist leaders to build a Soviet military base and staging area for the takeover of Central America. (At that time, Pat was still confident they could win.)

Just as Pat Buchanan was winding down his remarks, the president walked in and sat down about five chairs to my right. He welcomed us and told us his fight to bring democracy to Nicaragua was one of the toughest battles of his presidency. (At that time he had no way of knowing that his toughest fight still lay ahead.)

After the president's brief remarks I had a chance to speak up. "Mr. President," I said, "many of us are concerned that the American people are not getting the full truth about the situation in Central America. As a result, we feel sure that public opinion in this nation is being swayed."

President Reagan told me that his biggest frustration as president was his inability to get his side of the story out to the American people. "It seems that anything Daniel Ortega says is put on all the networks," he said, "but my statements are ignored." I could read the disappointment in his voice. "I am depending on sources like yours," he continued, "to give the rest of the story."

That is exactly what I attempted to do.

In his "kiss and tell" book, *Speaking Out,* former White House Press Secretary Larry Speakes clearly reveals that he was no friend to the Reagan policy on Central America. Yet even he recognized that the press had presented a one-sided view of the entire issue. Although his view of Ollie North was uncomplimentary, he did admit that public support for the president's policy "rose dramatically" after North's appearance on television during the congressional hearings in the summer of 1987. Here's how he put it:

> I think it was probably because the news media filtering prevented us from ever getting our message across. Atrocities committed by the other side never got the amount of publicity that our group got. . . . There was just a strong bias against American policy in Central America within the press corps. But once you removed the filter and had Ollie North speaking live and direct to the American people for a week, there was a dramatic change in public support for our Central American policy.[2]

All during the time President Reagan was struggling to keep Nicaragua from turning into another Soviet outpost like Cuba, the media continued their drumbeat of praise for the Communist Sandinistas and their lambasting of the people who were fighting for democracy. On and on, until I was sick of it, I read and heard the verbatim quotes of Daniel Ortega and his band of Merry Marxists telling us that they were simply trying to establish democracy for the people of Nicaragua.

One morning while reading the newspaper at my home, as is my usual custom before going to the studios for the broadcast, I read yet another story praising the Sandinistas for their courage in signing one of the many "peace plans" that were supposed to bring freedom and democracy to their land. I was still steaming when I went on the air. So on a whim, I decided to call the Nicaraguan Embassy in Washington—live on the air, mind you—and give them another side to the story.

"Point of View" Calls the Embassy

I had gotten their number before broadcast time. This day's program was "open line," so about thirty minutes into the show I told the audience just to hold on while I called the Nicaraguan Embassy. I dialed the number, and a man answered, "Nicaragua Embassy." I explained that we were "live" on the air and that I would like to talk to somebody about the newest peace plan. Well, after I was shunted around for a few minutes, a lady by the name of Sofia Clark came on the line.

I told her about "Point of View" and that we were broadcast live all across America. Then I said I wanted to talk to her about their Communist regime in Nicaragua. Immediately Sofia launched into the standard line about their goals being simply to give their people food, housing, a good education, and medical care.

That wasn't what I wanted to talk about. What I was interested in was the billions of dollars worth of Soviet weapons and armaments that were being shipped into Nicaragua.

"All we are doing," she stated, "is protecting our people from an invasion from the United States."

No surprise there. That's the "party line" answer I expected. So I moved on to asking about the ten-thousand-foot runway being built in their country, the one that could accommodate the largest of Soviet bombers.

"It's simply for the tourists," she told me.

Ah, yes, I should have realized. All those happy vacationers who are flooding in to see their glorious, war-torn land.

I had to take a commercial break, and while we were out for the two minutes I asked Sofia Clark if she would be willing to take some calls from people across America. She said she would. People certainly did want to talk to her. Before I even gave out the number, our entire phone bank was flashing.

Believe me, when we came back and told our listeners that Sofia Clark was available to talk with them, you would have thought they had been waiting for years to tell this woman and her cohorts just what they thought about their fiefdom down there in Nicaragua.

"Sounds like she has been well-schooled in some pretty overbearing tactics—just talking louder and louder to cover you up and going on and on to keep from having to respond to your questions," said Roy from Arizona.

"My blood runs cold when I hear you talk to this lady," Pat, a caller from Texas, told me.

Callers had their facts together—a deep-water port being built just across the border from Brownsville, Texas; Cuban troops seen building barracks close by; a Communist appointed head of the Subcommittee for Western Hemisphere Activities.

"What have the Russians promised you that would cause you to fall for what they're telling you?" Pat asked Sofia Clark. "You want freedom, yet anyone can see what has happened to Russian-controlled countries. Every bit of freedom is gone. What do you believe will happen to you?"

In reply Sofia talked of education for their children, rights to set their own rules for family, community, and country. "All we're asking is that people leave us alone," she said.

Our listeners proved to Sofia Clark that they knew more about Nicaraguan goals than they were given credit for. Many of them told her that she and her bosses shouldn't depend on the national left-liberal press to get a realistic reading on the American people. What the American people want, they told her, is for the Nicaraguan government to get their Communist dictatorship out of our backyard.

Evidently Sofia decided she'd had enough because she hung up on me. For a moment I sat quietly with only the sound of the empty dial tone going out over satellite all across America. What a ringing testimony that dial tone was to the fact that the Communist mind can't stand up to intelligent, rational dialogue.

Let me give you a brief footnote to this story: I got a letter from a man who told me he drives a truck for a living. As he pushes his eighteen wheeler across the nation, he tunes in to "Point of View." Sometimes he switches from one station to another in order to keep up with the show as he moves down the road. Sometimes, he told me, he hears the program two or three different times a day because some of the stations repeat it by tape delay in the evening or in the wee hours of the morning.

"Marlin," he told me, "when you called the Nicaraguan Embassy and caught them flatfooted, I was laughing so hard I almost ran off the road! They were so totally unprepared to answer the questions of the callers. I was so proud that somebody finally challenged them. I only wish you could have talked to Daniel Ortega himself.

"You should have seen me. I was pounding the steering wheel of my truck and yelling, 'Go get 'em, Marlin!' Go get 'em!'"

If we are to function and prosper in our society and if we are to make this a better place for our children and grandchildren, it is essential that we grasp the nature of the mass media. To do this, we must understand and accept that fact that a small, unelected, liberal elite own and control the media in our country.

Since we live and breathe in a society totally submerged in messages and sales pitches, biased news and information, entertainment with hidden messages, and outright propaganda—all of it beamed at us with space-age technology and unlimited funds, we must learn to cope with it and to inoculate ourselves and our families against its influence. If we can't handle it, we will surely be seduced by it.

Learning to cope is not an easy process. At times it's downright threatening. The problem is, we tend to be very comfortable with our long-held assumptions and behavior patterns.

We're in a battle. Make no mistake about it. And this battle for our minds will only be won through knowledge and prayer.

If you've read this far, you are aware of the problems and challenges we face.

Can you really make a difference? You bet you can!

WHAT CAN WE DO?

Spiro Agnew has been relegated to a footnote in history. Ask most young people who he is and you'll get a blank stare for your answer. Yet Spiro Agnew was the vice president of the United States during part of the Richard Nixon term. When his shady past caught up with him, he resigned his office in disgrace.

While he rightly deserved to be run out of office, Mr. Agnew's departure brought a large amount of glee to the elitists who control the national media. Why were they so glad to see him go? Because he was one of the very few politicians who have had the courage to say things about the media in such a way that Americans were beginning to believe him. (In his day, remember, television was relatively new and the TV newscast was just gaining a foothold.)

Spiro Agnew's broadside against the media came in a

speech he delivered in Des Moines, Iowa, on December 13, 1969. Here is part of what he had to say as quoted in *Spiro Agnew: Spokesman for America,* by Robert Curran:

> No medium has a more profound influence over public opinion. Nowhere in our system are there fewer checks on vast power. So nowhere should there be more conscientious responsibility exercised than by news media. The question is: are we demanding enough of television news presentations? And are the men of this medium demanding enough of themselves? . . . the purpose of my remarks tonight is to focus your attention on this little group of men who not only enjoy a right of instant rebuttal to every Presidential address, but more importantly, wield a free hand in selecting, presenting and interpreting the great issues of our nation.
>
> We cannot measure this power and influence by traditional democratic standards, for these men create national issues overnight. . . . For millions of Americans, the network reporter who covers a continuing issue . . . becomes in effect the presiding judge in a national trial by jury. . . . A raised eyebrow, an inflection of a voice, a caustic remark dropped in the middle of a broadcast can raise doubts in a million minds about the veracity of a public official or the wisdom of a government policy. . . .
>
> I am not asking for government censorship or any other kind of censorship. I am asking whether a form of censorship already exists when the news that 40 million Americans receive each night is determined by a handful of men responsible to their corporate employers and filtered through a handful of commentators who admit to their own set of biases. . . . We should never trust such power over public opinion in the hands of an elected government—it is time we questioned it in the hands of a small and unelected elite. The great networks have dominated America's airwaves for decades; the people are entitled to a full accounting of their stewardship.[3]

How are we to handle this almost all-pervasive news media we've got in America today? We can't just wait for them to go away. I posed this question to Dr. Marvin Olasky, author of *The Prodigal Press*. "How we are going to live with the news media?" I asked him.

"In the long run," he said, "we have to train Christian journalists. That's the thing that's really going to make a difference. Today, if newspapers and television and radio networks were owned by Christians who wanted to hire Christians, they would be hard pressed to fill those positions. We just haven't done enough training. That is one crucial area.

"In the short run, we have to be more discerning consumers of the news. Because if we are—if we can analyze and point out specific stories, then we can expose that specific type of media bias. That requires being able to recognize the tricks of the trade of journalism."

"What are some of those tricks of the trade?" I asked Dr. Olasky. "Can you be specific?"

He could.

"After giving a quote or two from both sides, a reporter will often bring in an expert," he said. "Watch closely. It will be those so-called experts who will indicate what the true position of the reporter is on the question. This is sometimes called 'journalistic ventriloquism.'

"Another trick is what is known as the 'talking head.' Someone just sitting there talking is much less effective than a graphic, visual demonstration. When something is shown, picture clear, charged emotionally, that can sway people. And of course, in the hands of someone who knows how to use them, pictures don't always tell the truth. They can be very carefully crafted propaganda—and they can be very effective."

I asked Dr. Olasky about his concern that more Christian young people get into journalism.

"In my mind that's the number one priority. But it has to be done in a very careful, thought-out way, one which involves really learning the tricks of the trade. Combine this with a Christian worldview and a knowledge of the techniques of journalism. And Christian journalists, the same as any others, have to 'pay their dues' and gain experience."

INTERPRETING COMMUNISM

CHAPTER 9

War of Words

"Here is my message. The main danger to America is not from Soviet-made nuclear warheads. Of course they are dangerous. But the main danger is the long, slow process of *demoralization*. It is a consistent effort which the KGB calls 'active measures.' Believe me, I know what I'm talking about. I was part of that process."

"Point of View" listeners were startled by this pronouncement from Thomas Schuman, a former member of the Novosti Press and a co-opted agent of the KGB. Mr. Schuman described in detail the Soviet tactics of "disinformation" and "active measures."

Born in Moscow in 1939, under the name Yuri Bezmenov, Thomas Schuman was the son of a senior officer of the Red Army's general staff. He graduated from the prestigious institute of oriental languages, specializing in the languages of India and Pakistan. Recruited by the KGB as a public relations officer, he spent several years in India, first as a translator with a Soviet economic aid group, then later as a press officer of the USSR embassy in New Delhi.

Fed up with the dirty business of KGB subversion and terrorism directed against the nations of Asia, Mr. Schuman, disguised as an American hippie, defected to the West. After traveling through India with a bunch of hashish-smoking kids, he was smuggled out of Bombay by the CIA,

147

flown to Athens where he was debriefed, given a new identity, and set free to land in Canada.

As Mr. Schuman says, "I was not a spy. Worse. I was an 'ideological subverter' for the KGB-controlled Novosti Press Agency (APN). Like a true-life Winston Smith from George Orwell's *1984*, I was working for the Communist equivalent of Orwell's Ministry of Truth. I manipulated the Western media. The term for this KGB effort is 'disinformation.'"

Soon after his immigration to Canada, Thomas Schuman told our radio audience that he became disillusioned with the Soviet system and planned for years to defect to the United States. When his opportunity for escape finally came, he arrived in America laden with secret documents that would once and for all prove to the West that the Soviets were indeed out to conquer the world.

One of the first places Mr. Schuman went to share his information was to the *New York Times*. But he found to his dismay that no one there would even talk to him. He was told to leave his phone number with the receptionist and they would call him—*if* they wanted to talk to him. He was never called.

On "Point of View," Mr. Schuman was finally getting his opportunity to warn Americans on a national broadcast, and he took full advantage of it. "Communist world aggression is a total war against humanity and human civilization," he said. "The driving force of this war of aggression is *ideology*. And an integral part of this war of ideology is *ideological subversion*, the process of changing the perception of reality in the minds of millions of people all over the world. The late comrade Andropov, the former head of the Soviet KGB, called this war of Communist aggression 'the final struggle for the minds and hearts of the people.'"

Thomas Schuman's is not an isolated voice. His message is reinforced by credible sources in the U.S. In 1983 testimony before the House Select Committee on Intelligence, Edward O'Malley, head of the FBI's intelligence division, said:

> The Soviets use the term 'active measures' to refer to operations intended to influence or otherwise affect other nations' policies. The basic aims of Soviet active measures are to weaken the opponents of the USSR and to create a favorable environment for the promotion of Soviet views and Soviet foreign policy objectives. The Kremlin continues to view the U.S. as the 'main enemy,' and most active measures are directed against American policies or American interests throughout the world.

I was recently told by another defector from the Soviet Union that there are over thirty thousand people working full time in disinformation operations and that their "number one theme is to try to convince the rest of the world, especially the free world, that the Soviets really aren't Communists any more."

About thirty minutes into our interview, Thomas Schuman handed me a magazine and asked me to look on a certain page. When I found the place, he said, "That article is the result of my work with Novosti Press in the Soviet Union."

Do you want to guess which magazine I was holding in my hand? It was the October 3, 1976, issue of *Look*. "It was one of their best pieces of disinformation to hit the United States," Mr. Schuman told me.

Let me tell you a bit about this "journalism." The cover was bannered "Russia Today," and the feature story was "The Soviets after Fifty Years." In lavish detail the article described how well the Communist system was working. In conclusion the *Look* article stated:

> If an honest, democratic election were held in the Soviet Union today, involving legitimate alternatives, sufficient time and opportunity for their exposure, and the assurance

that those elected would serve, the Communist Party would win. This is not speculation. It is a conclusion based upon on-the-spot observations and interviews by ten *Look* editors and photographers whose journeys through the Soviet Union for this issue total more than one year.

How did the *Look* journalists come up with such a positive conclusion? According to Mr. Schuman, they were only allowed to talk to preselected groups of people. "We found them; we washed them; we dressed them nicely, brushed their teeth, and told them what to say to the Americans."

This practice, he told us, is still in use today in the Soviet Union. It may not be obvious to American visitors, but all their encounters with Soviet citizens are prearranged by the KGB.

"Talking to a foreign correspondent is against the law," Mr. Schuman said. "You can get three years imprisonment for it."

I was shocked at what I was hearing. Evidently it showed on my face because Mr. Schuman quickly explained to me and the radio audience what had really happened. Here's what he told us:

"In 1965, I joined the Novosti Press Agency (Novosti means 'news' in Russian)—the biggest and most powerful propaganda, espionage, and ideological front of the KGB. After working a short time, I discovered that about 75 percent of the Novosti staffers were actually KGB officers; the other 25 percent were 'co-optees,' or KGB free-lance writers—informers like myself.

"The other interesting fact I discovered was that there was no 'news' at Novosti. My main job, apart from writing, editing, and translating propaganda materials to be planted in foreign media, was accompanying delegations of Novosti's guests—journalists, editors, publishers, writers, politicians, and businessmen—from foreign countries on tours of the USSR or to international conferences held in the Soviet Union.

"In actuality, as a free-lance journalist I did absolutely no writing or news coverage at all. My work with the KGB entailed combining my journalistic duties with the collection of intelligence data and the spreading of 'disinformation' to foreign countries for the purposes of Soviet propaganda and subversion."

The disinformation operation conducted against *Look* magazine was so successful that Mr. Schuman earned a bonus—a two-week, expense-paid trip to Italy.

Thomas Schuman's words are echoed by many who are trying to warn the United States. Arkady Schevchenko, former top advisor to Soviet Foreign Minister Andrei Gromyko, defected in April 1989 while serving as under-secretary-general of the United Nations. He too is speaking out. Mr. Schevchenko says that American Sovietologists (so-called Soviet experts) actually know very little about the Soviet Union.

In February 1985, Shevchenko told the National Press Club, "Unfortunately there are people who take for granted that there are independent thinkers in the Soviet Union who can inform them properly. This is not true." He says the Soviet government will deliberately allow some citizens to inform foreign correspondents on nonessential matters, such as Chernenko's illness. "What they say is partly true, but they are actually disinforming the Sovietologists. Anybody in the Soviet Union who talks to them is acting on the instructions of the Soviet government. It is all government controlled."

While Thomas Schuman was in the studio with me, he showed me a May 1983 article in *BYU Today,* a magazine from Brigham Young University. In the article Dr. Gary Browning, who visited the Soviet Union, echoed the 1967 *Look* magazine refrain: if free elections were held in the Soviet Union, the Communists would win. Even though

Browning admits he was accompanied by Novosti Press agents on his trip, he refused to believe he was controlled or duped.

Recent Soviet disinformation operations have focused on arms control and disarmament, and the KGB has concentrated on promoting the nuclear freeze and peace movements. The World Peace Council, the largest international Soviet front organization, has been directly involved in organizing and mobilizing the peace movement in the United States.

On "Point of View," Thomas Schuman confirmed reports that Romesh Chandra, head of the World Peace Council, is a Communist and an ideological agent for the KGB. "Yes, I helped him many times in India," Mr. Schuman told me. "Chandra owes his influence to the Soviet propaganda system. He was a nobody until we promoted him."

Further into the interview, Mr. Schuman explained that he held the position of press officer of the USSR embassy in India when he defected in 1970, shortly before the Bangladesh crisis. "My motivation to defect was very simple," he said. "First, I was morally disgusted with the Communist system. There are millions of people in my country who hate the system which Ronald Reagan accurately describes as the evil empire. That is exactly what it is.

"Second, I had no doubt that the United States, with its free-market, capitalist system, was the best system in the world. It is the most productive and the most unique system in the history of mankind. The greatest proof is that people run to America, not away from it."

Mr. Schuman's actual defection was precipitated by the Soviet subversion of East Pakistan, a move orchestrated by the Soviet embassy in India. The Bangladesh crisis was not a grassroots revolution, he told us. It was a

Soviet invasion of East Pakistan, an invasion that made use of the Indian army.

Thomas Schuman personally observed the arrival of revolutionaries trained in Moscow at the Patrice Lumumba University. "This is the KGB-controlled center which trains the professional assassins your media politely called 'leaders of the national liberation movement.' We secretly called them left-wing death squads. You never see this expression in the *New York Times,* of course, because they are very concerned about right-wing death squads."

An exciting thing was happening. All across America, via radio waves, Thomas Schuman was pulling away the shroud of secrecy that so effectively keeps us from seeing the inner working of the "evil empire."

Mr. Schuman continued his story: It was when the imported revolutionaries arrived to infiltrate East Pakistan and turn it into a Soviet satellite, he said, that he decided to defect. Disguised as a hippie, he joined a group of long-haired, bearded, and barefoot Americans who were in India seeking "enlightenment."

"My specific purpose in defecting," he said, "was to bring the message of impending danger to the United States. I wanted to tell the free world to wake up and stop this madness!"

The result? At the time, not many people listened to him. In the last decade, however, more defectors from the Soviet Union have corroborated Mr. Schuman's story. More and more, the danger of Soviet disinformation is being brought into the open.

Disinformation is one of the chief weapons in the Soviet war of subversion against the United States.

The Four Stages of Subversion

Mr. Schuman described what he called the four stages of subversion. "The first stage, *demoralization,* takes from fifteen to twenty years. This is the amount of time required to educate at least one generation of students, to expose them to the Marxist ideology of centralized government." (As I listened to him speak, I couldn't help thinking of Cuba and Nicaragua.) During the demoralization stage, he told us, the basic institutions of society—including religion, education, and the media—are attacked.

The second stage of subversion is *destabilization*. This lasts five years or less. "At this stage the KGB narrows their efforts to the essentials: defense, the economy, diplomacy, and the internal political process of the country."

Destabilization leaves the country on the verge of a crisis. "And this is the third stage—" he told us, "*crisis.* This can be effected through three basic methods: civil war, revolution, or invasion. But the result is always the same—a closed society."

The last stage of subversion, we were told, is *normalization*. This is where they make an effort to produce a normal state of socialism. "In other words, borders are closed, the media are censored, and the opposition are executed. In this stage, the human being becomes the property of the state. His basic right to be alive and free, his right to the pursuit of happiness, is no longer given by God as stated in the American Constitution. In the 'normalized' socialist state, rights are given only by the government."

As I listened attentively to what this man was saying, one question loomed in my mind: just where are we in our battle for survival? So I asked, "Mr. Schuman, where is America in this cycle of subversion?"

Thomas Schuman looked across the interview table and straight into my eyes. "Mr. Maddoux," he said, "fifteen years ago I thought America was approaching the crisis stage. But after traveling as a lecturer across the United States, I have changed my opinion. I think America is not even demoralized."

Not only did Thomas Schuman see things in our country that gave him cause for hope, but he also sensed a new feeling of self-confidence and self-respect in millions of Americans, a genuine conviction that our system is indeed the best system.

Mr. Schuman said, "Some 'intellectuals,' some crazy characters in Hollywood, some educational and union figureheads may be demoralized, but the United States republic is firmly patriotic. There is great hope for America."

What a message from one in a position to know!

When I asked Mr. Schuman what he had gained personally from his defection from the USSR to the United States, he told me, "Materially, I have gained nothing. What I *have* gained is a firm commitment to the United States as the last real frontier of freedom. This country will be the last to be 'liberated' by Marxists, socialists, and domestic 'do-gooders.'"

I don't think Thomas Schuman looks at all like an international spy. Certainly he's not from the mold of the fictional character James Bond (007). Yet I found it difficult to tie him in with his story of mystery, danger, and intrigue without hearing the guns firing and feeling his cold fears as he tried to escape the Soviets.

It was at this point, while I was lost in my own thoughts, that Mr. Schuman looked at me intently and said—almost pleadingly, I thought—"Mr. Maddoux, if the 'liberationists' succeed in bringing their 'new order' to America, chances are you and I will meet in front of a firing squad—or worse, in a 'reeducation' forced labor camp in the 'Alaskan Peoples' Democratic Republic.'"

Unlike Thomas Schuman, I am not and never have been in the business of "disinformation." My business is communicating truthful information to the best of my ability.

As a broadcaster—a radio journalist—my work is dealing with words, ideas, thoughts, worldviews. I love words. They are powerful tools—both for good and for evil. Words convey ideas, and ideas have consequences. Words help to form our opinions and our worldview.

Sometimes when I'm writing or preparing for my broadcast, I'll search through my entire mental file cabinet of vocabulary—perhaps I'll consult a dictionary or two as well—just to find that one word that best expresses my precise thought.

I always notice the words people use and how language frames the issues we discuss. I enjoy people who express themselves clearly and concisely. Any person who can use a few words powerfully rather than weaken the point with excess verbiage has my admiration.

Over the past several years and thousands of hours of broadcasting, after interviewing hundreds of people and listening to the results of their research and experiences, I have arrived at some definite conclusions about the meaning of our earthly existence and the life-and-death issues we face each day. One of my conclusions is that we as a nation are in a battle—a war—for our very survival as a free people. If we remain a free people on into the twenty-first century, it only will be because we have become better informed on the forces at war in our country and better informed as to what a loss will mean.

I have interviewed many people who have left their Communist homelands to come to America, and, without exception, they sound the same alarm. What they tell my listeners and me is that the same forces that undermined their own countries are right now at work in the United States of America.

The Soviet Communists are trying to control us. There is a war going on in this nation. It's a battle for our minds, our attentions, our thoughts. The battle being waged is one to control nations by capturing the national mind-set.

When Mr. Schuman was telling us about his disinformation job, he stated that the Soviets were confident of winning the war against America. And confident that they could do it without firing a shot. They would win the war of words, of propaganda. They would win the battle for our minds.

"The highest art of war is not to fight at all," Mr. Schuman told us, "but to subvert your enemy by destroying his moral principles, his religion, his culture, and the traditional links between individuals and society. When a country is demoralized, you can take it over painlessly, without firing a shot."

His statement brought to my mind the words of the Chinese philosopher Sun-Tzu who in the year 500 BC wrote in his book *The Art of War:* "All warfare is based primarily on deception of an enemy. Fighting on a battlefield is the most primitive way of making war. There is no art higher than to destroy your enemy without a fight—by subverting anything of value in the enemy's country. All warfare is based on deception. . . . his primary target is the mind of the opposing commander." Sun-Tzu realized that an indispensable preliminary to battle was to attack the mind of the enemy.

Every time I finish conducting an interview with someone who has lived under a repressive government and then comes to our country to live, someone who has a desire to warn the American people, I go away from the studio and ask myself, "Could it really be possible for someone to subvert such a freedom-loving nation as America? Could anyone truly move an entire nation away from its original goals, its values, and its religion?"

That's when I remember the power of words. And the power of the media. And who the people who control the media are. And what their beliefs are. And the plan they have for our country.

And then I have to admit that, yes, it could indeed happen. An entire nation of people could be led into slavery, all the while believing they were still in control of their own lives. The skillful use of words makes it possible.

To Conquer a Nation . . .

In order to conquer a nation without military action, some very basic steps must be taken:

First, the moral high ground must be seized. This is best done by capturing the language. The language is then controlled by changing the meaning of words so that the preferred cause is perceived by the citizens to be the moral one. The media make the perfect place to begin a language change.

Second, the flow of information must be controlled. For, you see, people base their decisions upon the information they have. If the receivers only get the information certain people want them to have, their decisions will be virtually predetermined. The media are our main source of information.

Third, the avenues of communication must be monopolized. The most effective means of conveying information and ideas include the schools, the arts, the entertainment industry, music, and such media sources as radio, television, and the printed page.

Demagogues have known for thousands of years that when a person or a group of people or a government control these avenues to people's minds, they will then be able to tell the public what to think and how to think about it. They can tell the people which group or governmental system, which political or military leader or politburo or revolutionary group, which religion or set of values to hate and which to love and embrace.

By controlling these things, a person is not only in a position to deliver his message, but at the same time he can censor out the messages of those who disagree with him. In this way he can gradually change the nation simply by withholding information, shutting out opposing views, and showcasing the views he wants accepted.

The result is that the people are convinced that they are making intelligent decisions when in reality they are thinking precisely what those in control want them to think. A nice arrangement for one who would take over and control, don't you think?

In Communist countries such as Russia, Cuba, China, and Nicaragua, the task is accomplished by governmental control over all these persuasive tools, especially the media. The government shuts out by force all opposing views and bombards the populace with the "big lie" until people are finally beaten into mental submission. Even those who don't agree with the government end up going along out of sheer weariness. We saw this happen over and over again as our young men succumbed to Communist brainwashing in Korea and Vietnam.

After a generation or two of totalitarian propaganda and the exclusion of outside information, those in power are able to raise a generation of young people who have no point of reference other than that which their masters have force fed them.

At the present time, the government of the United States of America is forbidden by law to broadcast propaganda to the people of this country. Since it's the law of the land, most people feel secure that they are not the subjects of ideological warfare. Nothing could be further from the truth. The fact is, we *are* being subjected to intense persuasion through our mass media. The only difference is that it is being accomplished in a more subtle form.

As President Lyndon Johnson has been reported to have said about the escalation of the Vietnam War, "Seduction is slower than rape, but it's just as effective." One cannot change the moral consensus of a nation overnight. That would be tantamount to rape. But that same one can "seduce" a nation by controlling the language, the flow of information via the media, and the other avenues to the minds of the people.

An incredible thing has happened in America within the last few decades. Have you noticed the subtle change that has occurred in our language? It's there. For all practical purposes, our language has been captured by the secularists and has been changed to reflect the "new morality." Certain words have mysteriously disappeared from our vocabulary while others have come to mean something altogether different from what they meant in the not-too-distant past.

"Point of View" listeners were treated to a philosophical feast when Joseph Sobran stopped by the studio to chat. Mr. Sobran is a nationally syndicated columnist and senior editor of *National Review,* the premier publication of the conservative movement.

I shared my concern over the changing nature of our language with Mr. Sobran. I told him I believed the American people were being seduced by the clever use of language. Then I asked him point-blank if he honestly felt our national media were biased. His answer should be heard by every man and woman in America. Here's what he said:

> If they kept [bias] out of their reporting, it would be no problem. But if they have a sense of mission to reform society, as so many of them do, then they will reform it along the lines of their ideals.
>
> You see a lot more skepticism about our government sometimes than you do about a Communist government. You certainly see a lot more skepticism about right-wing dictatorships than about Communist ones. The Communists are always referred to as leaders, as if they have followers. "Soviet leader," "Cuban leader," "Chinese leader." I even saw "Polish leader"—right after martial law was imposed. The *New York Times* ran a story about Brezhnev visiting Poland, and there was a picture of him with General Jarulzelski, and the caption said: "The Soviet leader met

with the Polish leader." You see this prejudice time and again.

We really saw the adversary press develop, I think, in the Johnson administration in reaction to one side of his policies. Johnson was anti-Communist internationally, and he was socialist at home. The media attacked the right-wing foreign policy. So the adversary media are only adversary toward the right-wing tendencies of any president. They will criticize any president for being insufficiently leftist.

WHAT CAN WE DO?

I told Mr. Sobran I had read one of his columns entitled, "Words [Dan] Rather Can't Say."

"Can you tell us about it?" I asked.

That column, he said, was his way of showing how language was being controlled in the national media. Then he proceeded to give us example after example of how pervasive this philosophical censorship is in our own American media.

"There are certain words," he said, "that are the new cultural and political taboos. It's unlikely that even Dan Rather could get away with saying them. For instance, you won't hear an anchorman refer to the 'international Communist conspiracy.' Without a doubt, Communism is an international movement, yet the American media will no more tolerate a reference to the 'international Communist conspiracy' than it will tolerate a reference to the 'free world'—another taboo phrase.

"Young people no longer 'fornicate.' That would be a 'judgmental' way to put it. Instead, they are 'sexually active.' And, of course, nobody on television dares refer to homosexuality as a 'perversion' or as 'sodomy.' Homosexuals are now 'gays.'

"'Unborn baby' is another unmentionable. It has become a 'fetus.' And it can no longer be 'killed'; abortion merely 'terminates a pregnancy.' 'God' and 'Jesus' are, of course, unmentionable. But they use plenty of words with strong moral implications: racism, sexism, discrimination, corruption, repression."

I found Mr. Sobran to be one of the most fascinating guests I have ever interviewed. His insight into the mind-set of our national media was thorough and knowledgeable. He concluded by telling us, "It is pretty clear from the entire pattern that the left wing of American politics and culture has acquired a dictatorial veto power over the vocabulary of television. No word it objects to will survive that medium.

"Censorship? Not exactly. What has happened is that the left has managed to transmute its ideology into a form of etiquette, or more specifically, into rules of verbal behavior. Whatever offends the left is offensive. Never mind that television constantly offends conservative sensibilities. The left writes the rules without assistance, thank you. Etiquette has this advantage over public debate: it leaves no room for disagreement. Gradually, the conservative point of view and its natural vocabulary are ruled out of bounds on grounds of taste."

Next time you hear a newscaster use some of these phrases, do a doubletake. Question everything else in that particular story. Beware of other reports from this same journalist. In your mind, substitute unborn baby for fetus so that you can see the real implications of the action. And, of course, you may notice close parallels between our media's manipulation of words and truth and the world of the future as seen by George Orwell. Frightening similarities, don't you think?

Orwell wrote in his book, *1984:*

> Winston sank his arms to his sides and slowly refilled his lungs with air. . . . His mind slid away into the . . . world of Doublethink. To know and not to know. . . . To hold simul-

taneously two opinions which cancelled out, knowing them to be contradictory and believing in both of them to use logic against logic—to repudiate morality while laying claim to it. . . . Even to understand the word "doublethink" involved the use of "doublethink."

Even the names of the four ministries by which we are governed exhibit a sort of impudence in their deliberate reversal of facts. The Ministry of Peace concerns itself with war. The Ministry of Truth, with lies; the Ministry of Love, with torture; the Ministry of Plenty, with starvation. These contradictions are not accidental, nor do they result from 'ordinary' hypocrisy. They are deliberate exercises in Doublethink.[1]

Welcome to 1984.

CHAPTER 10

We Rescue the Evil Empire—Again

Communism is a monumental failure. The Soviet economy is in a shambles, and the entire system is being threatened from within. The arms race has bankrupted the Soviet Union. The very thought of trying to keep up with the United States in our Strategic Defense Initiative program throws the Soviets into terrible inner turmoil. Were they to become involved in as expensive a competition as that, they would never be able to hold onto their power over the Russian people—and they know it.

So how do they manage to survive? Only one way—with the life-saving infusions of money from Western capitalists. That's the key. That is what their whole public relations campaign is about—Western money.

Here is the way Larry Abraham explained it to "Point of View" listeners: "The issue at stake, now and in the future, is not European-based intermediate range ballistic missiles. That is only a straw man. The real issue is aid and trade. It is about selling, lending, supporting, building, and transferring money, credit, and technology (and more of your tax dollars, by the way) to bail out the Soviets once again."

One of the big problems shared by most Americans, whether media promoters or media consumers, is that they just don't understand the Communist mind. The point we

164

must clearly understand is this: Marxist-Leninists are still convinced that Communism is going to be brought about.

Clark Bowers, director of the Claremont Institute's Commission on US-USSR Relations, described to "Point of View" listeners the four themes Gorbachev has been pushing—and, I might add, pushing extremely successfully.

THEMES OF COMMUNIST DOUBLETALK

The first theme is this: There are good Communists and there are bad Communists. Right now a struggle is under way between the good and the bad. Guess who the leader of the good Communists is? The Soviet dove who so badly wants peace? Right! Mikhail Gorbachev himself.

The end result of this first theme is clear: If there are good Communists struggling against bad Communists, we had better do everything we possibly can to make sure we keep a good Communist in power. We can start by making him *Time* magazine's "Man of the Year." Of course, making certain his projects and reform movements succeed may mean the Western world will have to give him $32 million a day. But, hey, if that's what's needed, that's what we'll have to do.

Gorbachev's second theme emerges from the fact that Soviet policymakers finally understand that the American mind is much different from the Soviet mind. The Soviet mind says it is always better to give the appearance of being stronger and mightier than an opponent, that it's always negative to appear weak or helpless. So in the past, even when their economy was in real trouble—as it is today and always has been—they have tried to make it look as if it were working.

Now, however, they're beginning to understand the American mentality. When we see an enemy or a sick dog or anything weak and helpless, two things happen: first we are consumed by a desperate desire to reach out and help the poor thing; then we search for ways we can blame ourselves for its terrible condition.

So what are the Soviets doing now? Why, releasing depressing information, of course—showing us they are the ones in distress. They are giving out material that confirms what some conservatives have been saying all along, that Marxist economics is a colossal failure. What a perfect way to get our sympathy—and our help.

The third theme—and the one that has probably been the most successful of all—says it isn't the differing moral visions or the separate political systems that have caused problems between our two countries. What has actually caused the problems is the arms themselves. The tactic here, you see, is this: if they can frame the issue so that arms themselves appear to be the problem, then any country that acquires arms is contributing to the problem.

An extension of this reasoning goes this way: There is no difference between a police officer and a kidnapper. They both have guns, don't they? They both walk around at night; they both go into the houses of people who don't want them. Peacekeeper, lawbreaker—what's the difference, really?

When we focus on arms as the source of tension, then all we have to do is reduce arms and we'll reduce the tension. That's what they say. And many Americans are believing it.

The fourth and final theme has to do with semantics. Gorbachev has been harnessing American words that sound wonderful to us, but which have an entirely different meaning to him and his people. For instance, he has been focusing a great deal on the beloved American concept of *democracy.* As a matter of fact, democracy has been one of Mr. Gorbachev's favorite words. When Clark Bowers asked the Soviets if by democracy they meant the Jeffersonian democracy we Americans believe in, they hemmed and hawed and hesitated. Finally they admitted that no, that wasn't what they meant.

So what *do* they mean? Well, by democracy they mean greater discussion is allowed all the way from the lower levels on up to the top levels. Once a decision has been reached at any level above you, however, that decision is completely and totally binding on all the lower levels. Not only must everyone comply with what is dictated, but everyone must also claim that that decision is truly and wholeheartedly believed in each one's own heart of hearts. And each one must follow that course without question and without dissent.

Although the Soviets are clearly pursuing the same goals they have always pursued, one pivotal element has changed: in order to achieve their goals, they now desperately need the financial help of Western capitalists. And so they have dressed Mikhail and Raisa in acceptable attire and sent them off to "do business" with the Western governments, Western bankers, and supranational corporation bosses.

Their "business" is to tap Western capital. Now, we're not just talking about a little money here. We're talking about a *lot* of money. Currently the Soviets are borrowing $700 million *per month!* Without those loans, they cannot hope to gain the hard currency they need if they are ever to recover from their worst economic slump since the 1920s.

And they are finding willing and able partners, too. These partners are Western bankers who have been rocked by multibillion-dollar losses from loans they made to Third World nations.

David Funderburk, former U.S. ambassador to Rumania, joined us on "Point of View" to tell America what led up to his stepping down from his post in protest of U.S. policy toward Communist Rumania and Eastern Europe.

His story is recorded in his excellent book, *Pinstripes and Reds*.

Ambassador Funderburk told us of the difficulties faced by anyone who dared challenge the aid-to-Communists policy of the state department. He told how courageous dissidents are let down by United States policy-makers and diplomats. And he explained the ways in which the state department actually cooperates with some of the world's most ruthless Communists.

This book by Ambassador Funderburk is the first account by an American ambassador to a Soviet bloc country to document the collaboration between the leadership elite of the state department and Rumanian Communists.

"I think we're propping up Communist regimes which are bankrupt and corrupt and would fall without our aid," Ambassador Funderburk told us. "It's economic aid from the U.S. government, from big business, and from the big banks in America that is helping to save the Communist system. As President Reagan's ambassador to Communist Rumania, I saw firsthand the Pinstripers and Reds working together."

They know what they're doing. Someone is confused, but it's not the Soviets.

It should be fairly obvious to any clear-thinking American that the Kremlin reads the *New York Times*, the *Washington Post*, and *Time* magazine; that they view the three major networks and monitor the so-called peace movement and the antinuclear activists; and that they have mammoth files on people they can use as "useful idiots" (a phrase coined by none other than Lenin himself).

The moment Gorbachev's plane (I call it Trojan Horse One) landed in Washington, he knew exactly whom he wanted to see and what he wanted to discuss. Seeing the American president was only a small part of his agenda. This man didn't want to see Disneyland; he had more important things on his mind. His frontmen, both from Russia and right here in the United States, had arranged for dozens of clandestine meetings with politicians, businessmen, bankers, media people, comrades, and fellow travelers. And as you may remember, many of America's rich, famous, and most powerful people paid homage to the Communist dictator.

On the "CBS Evening News," Dan Rather reported: "Gorbachev had more on his agenda today than Afghanistan or Ronald Reagan. The Soviet General Secretary Gorbachev wasted no Summit time, meeting with 'movers and shakers' outside the White House, just about anyone who would listen. The leader of the Kremlin got together with the leaders of Congress—on his own turf—the Soviet Embassy.

"Gorbachev also found time to bring his own brand of Glasnost to lunch at the state department and directly to media representatives, playing every bit the Soviet leader who knows the image he wants to project to the 'Global Village.'"

And in a photo session with President Reagan at the White House, CBS reported, "Perhaps one of the most telling moments, the White House photo opportunity, Gorbachev did all the talking."

During his visit, the press gave Gorbachev what he wanted. And they ran their own surveys to prove how well liked and trusted he was. Throughout the entire event, I had the feeling that everything went along exactly as the KGB planned it. As for our own press, they were all too willing to cooperate.

The CBS report continued by saying, "Gorbachev is sophisticated enough to know how American opinion is shaped, so this afternoon he met with a 'select' group of publishers and broadcasters." When the subject of human rights came up during this meeting with hand-picked opinionmakers, Gorbachev showed his true colors when he angrily lashed out at them saying, "What moral right does

America have to assume the pose of a teacher? Who has given it the right to teach us moral lessons? I told the president yesterday, 'Mr. President, you are not the prosecutor, and I am not the accused.'"

Revealing little outburst, don't you think?

Remember, one of the principal things Mikhail Gorbachev is attempting to gain is moral equivalence. He wants his atheistic, Communist regime to be legitimated in the eyes of the civilized world. He wants us to forget about the millions they have murdered and the repressive nature of their system and to simply accept them—without any changes on their part.

A. M. Rosenthal wrote that Gorbachev has pursued not just arms treaties but another, even greater, prize: "It is nothing less than achieving, in the eyes of the world, full moral equality with the United States. Gorbachev's brilliant strategy is to attain this goal without essentially changing the system upon which the Soviet dictatorship and his own power rest. . . . It is hugely important to Moscow that the world believe there is no great difference between us."

He went ahead to warn, "Moral equality erodes our own values and visions and compassion; that is its greatest danger. . . . There can be no moral equality between a democracy and a dictatorship, even a dictatorship with velvet on the bars."[1]

It was this quest for moral equivalence between Western civilization and the Communist system that was behind Gorbachev's arrogant question: "What moral right does America have to assume the pose of a teacher?" And, of course, the national media helped him along in his hypocritical posturing by featuring him on the evening news.

You see, totalitarian states such as the Soviet Union can parcel out protected monopolies to whomever they please without having to worry about labor unions or congresses or strikes or boycotts. The Soviet elite control the economy all the way from research and development to manufacturing, sales, delivery, and price setting. It is the government that owns and controls all phases of business.

So, if the politburo grants an American industrialist a monopoly on the manufacture and sale of pencils, for example, he doesn't have to worry about competition. His company is the only foreign company allowed to sell pencils in the entire Soviet Union.

Multinational corporations love doing business that way. And it's very easy to shut out the moans of the suffering millions when you fly your own company jet to Moscow, are whisked through the streets in a government-sponsored motorcade, then check into a luxury hotel to live and dine with the dictators in opulent splendor. And the KGB *guarantees* that protesters and "troublemakers" will not bother you during your stay. Sounds pretty good, doesn't it?

So that's the bottom line. The international bankers and industrialists from the United States are drooling from their collective greedy mouths to go into business with the Communists. It's all a question of profit.

I've had a number of guests who have talked about "the establishment" here in America and its connection to such organizations as the Council on Foreign Relations (CFR) and the Trilateral Commission. While I may not totally agree with them that there is a small cadre of sinister individuals who meet together and plan wars, famines, and general mayhem, I do agree that there are extremely powerful people in America who have a very definite agenda that's not in the best interests of freedom. These are people who have enormous wealth and who exert immense influence on the government, on tax-exempt foundations, on the universities, on the news media, and on the entertainment industry.

Whether or not you subscribe to the "conspiracy" theory of history, it is a fact that a good deal of Wall Street money is involved in trade with the Soviets, in the control of the national media, and in the running of foreign affairs. If a New Age of Detente dawns, these same money interests stand to reap billions from propping up the Soviet system. And, believe me, you can expect them to see to it that detente and the Soviet Union get favorable coverage on the evening news.

Unfortunately, American big business sees the Soviet Union as possessing enormous potential for megaprofits. And as we have seen, it's easy to deal with dictatorships—of the left or the right—because once a deal has been struck, there is no competition with other companies. International bankers and industrialists simply sit down with the Communist party bosses, dance to the party tune, toast the Great Leaders of the Socialist Republics of the world, and reap lucrative monopolies for their companies. Oh yes—they also have to promise not to "say anything bad" about international Communism on the television or radio networks nor in the newspapers and magazines they might happen to own or control.

Even though the Soviet Union has been stealing American technology for decades, there's a good deal it doesn't have to steal. That's because there are plenty of American businessmen and international companies who are all too willing to sell the Soviets whatever they need—for a handsome profit, naturally.

Senator Malcolm Wallop (R-WY) pointed out that Soviet indebtedness to the West is estimated to be at least $100 billion, but only the Soviets know for sure. It seems that Western loans to Soviet-owned banks located in the West are not included in calculations of gross Soviet indebtedness. The Soviets are able to maintain their buying power because of loans of $8-10 billion in new "untied" loans—made within the last two years alone.

Eighty percent of the loans to the Soviets are "untied," meaning they are not restricted to any particular project or program. It's fairly obvious that the Soviets are using this hard currency to buy Western technology and to support their military machinery.

M. Stanton Evans wrote an article entitled "Tech Transfer: The Next Big Issue?" which appeared in *Human Events,* March 7, 1987. Evans' article blew the whistle on the massive transfer of vital information and technology to the Soviet Union. He said that although it could turn out to be the most important foreign policy issue of the decade, the story has not received the publicity it deserves. He calls it a somewhat incredible process in which the United States and other Western nations have systematically built up the military-industrial power of the Communists.

Evans goes on to say that we have been conducting an arms race against ourselves and that if certain business and political interests have their way, we will continue to do so in the future.

These kinds of dealings remind me of when I was a kid, before World War II. My family lived in southeast Texas in a small "sawmill town" called Honey Island. My dad and Uncle Simon worked at Kirby Lumber Company sawmill for $1.60 a day. We lived in a company house and shopped at the company store.

Times were rough for our families, but one of the ways I could pick up a little spending money was to gather scrap metal and sell it to a man who came around in a truck each week. It was only after the outbreak of the war that I learned that the scrap metal I sold to him was being shipped to Japan. The scrap metal that a few thousand other kids in America and I had sold was used to make the shells for the Japanese cannons that killed American soldiers.

Someday nuclear missiles may rain down on the United States, missiles that were built with the technology Western industrialists sold to the Soviet Union. And what will their millions of profits mean then?

Lenin had a clear insight into the greed of some Western businessmen when he wrote that they would "sell us the rope to be used to hang them." It's not just rope that's being sold. It's satellite technology, computer technology, weapons technology, guidance systems for Soviet missiles, and anything else the Russians haven't already arranged to steal.

Alexandr Solzhenitsyn tried to warn us. In an article titled "The Matter of Dr. Armand Hammer," printed in the *Conservative Digest* in December, 1987, he is quoted as saying:

> There is an alliance between our Communist leaders and you capitalists. The alliance is not new. The very famous Armand Hammer, who is flourishing here today, laid the basis for this when he made the first exploratory trip into Russia, still in Lenin's time, in the very first years of the Revolution. He was extremely successful in this . . . mission and since that time . . . we observe continuous and steady support by the businessmen of the West and of the Soviet Communist leaders. Their clumsy and awkward economy, which could never overcome its own difficulties by itself, is continually getting material and technological assistance. . . . And if today the Soviet Union has powerful military and police forces—they are used to crush our movement for freedom in the Soviet Union—[we] have Western capital to thank for this also.

When someone from the newsroom handed me the wire copy of a story that said President Bush had just "pardoned" Armand Hammer, I thought of these words of Solzhenitsyn. Hammer, you may remember, had pleaded guilty in 1976 to three counts of making illegal campaign contributions, totaling $54,000, to President Nixon's 1972 reelection campaign.

An article in *Human Events* (August 26, 1989) expressed the paper's displeasure with the pardon saying that many would recall Hammer's seventy years of dutiful service on behalf of the Soviet Union with Russia's Communist leaders who "have done their best to enrich him while advancing an agenda all their own." For Hammer has not only been a business partner of the Soviets; he has been a pro-Soviet propagandist par excellence since the days of Lenin, and he could—and still can—always be counted on to "voice the Soviet line to ill-informed Westerners and to put the best face on Soviet brutality."

A pardon for Ollie North? Forget it! But a full pardon for a man who has regularly trafficked with the Communists. While Lenin was liquidating millions of people, Hammer was conducting "business as usual." I guess the moral of the story is that it's only treason when you help the side that's fighting for freedom and human dignity.

Our Schools Don't Help

Parents, be constantly on guard for programs of propaganda whereby Soviet Russia is being pushed in our public schools. While painting Gorbachev as a "new" kind of leader and the USSR as a less dangerous adversary, the Soviets will surely be pushing programs of internationalism and pacifism.

Did you know that part of the package we got out of the Reagon-Gorbachev treaties was a program for an expansion of exchanges of school curriculum? The Soviets and their fellow travelers in the U.S. know that if they are going to "Sovietize" the United States, they must do it through the children. In our exchange of teachers, curricula, textbooks, and students, I think you know who is going to get the short end of the stick. I guarantee it won't be the Soviets.

The overload of propaganda is already beginning in many of our school textbooks. For example, in a book put out by D.C. Heath and Company called *The World to Present,* Siberia is touted as the "land of opportunity and adventure." It also says that the Soviet-captive nations of Bulgaria, Rumania, Albania, and Poland are "independent" nations. And in this textbook—and in our national media as well—Mikhail Gorbachev is called President Reagan's "counterpart."

No, Mr. Gorbachev is not our president's counterpart. The United States president is the freely elected president of a free country. Mr. Gorbachev is the head henchman of a slave state.

Another place where America is going to come in last is in the exchange of students and educators. While Soviet students and educators have been drilled since kindergarten in the fundamentals of Marxist-Leninist ideology and dialectical materialism, American students know little or nothing about the fundamentals of freedom. And they certainly know nothing about Marxist-Leninist thought, the driving force behind that barbaric regime. Furthermore, American students have been taught that the Soviet system is the "moral equivalent" to our own.

So how will the American kid hold his or her own against a well-trained doctrinaire Marxist? The answer is easy—the American kid won't.

To make matters worse, our children are being taught that the tensions between America and the Soviet Union are simply "prejudices" and "misunderstandings," that there really is no substantial difference between us.

Of course we all want a world free of war. But this is not the way to achieve it. What this kind of propaganda adds up to is "surrender on the installment plan."

While the leftist media bombard you with encouragement to embrace this wonderful new "leader," remember that your kids are being systematically programmed to accept the concept of a one-world government. And it's being done in your tax-financed public schools.

Ah, the one-world government. While we're being told that many of us still carry around the excess "baggage" of nationalism and love of country, the establishment has been pushing us toward this governmental ideal. It was tried first with the League of Nations, then later with the United Nations. Now the buzzword is "INTERdependence."

Several years ago, many of our politicians went so far as to sign a Declaration of INTERdependence. Our nation's school textbooks are full of it, urging our children to divert their loyalties toward the "world community." The misguided hope is that the West will adopt more "progressive" ideas and become more collectivist (socialist) so that we can "converge" with a more amiable Soviet Union.

When I see pictures on American television of Armand Hammer and other American industrialists and state department officials walking arm in arm with Mikhail Gorbachev and the other Kremlin bosses in Moscow, I am deeply disturbed. These people are being given the royal treatment by the Communists, and the pictures are being shown on the nightly news to a very gullible American public.

In order for the American public to sit silently while our government and big businesses enter into partnership with the Soviets, the American perception of Communism must be changed. Now, understand, *Communism* itself doesn't have to change. It's our *perception* of Communists and the Communist ideology that must change if their plan is to work.

We should applaud when the Soviets recognize the human rights of their people. But, remember, the Communist Party is still in charge and the new freedoms are only a loan. They can be taken away just as quickly as they were given.

Big money is at stake here, and it all depends upon whether or not the American people buy the Soviet "sell job." So far, they are proving to be excellent salespeople.

So let's encourage the Soviet Union to abandon their totalitarian regime and move toward true democracy. But we shouldn't finance it!

WHAT CAN WE DO?

For most of the early years of my Christian life I was taught that my "spiritual" development was the most important thing and that I should not entangle myself with "the things of the world." Unfortunately, the entanglement with "the world" included such things as politics, public policy, national morality, government, voting, the arts, entertainment, and a host of other destiny shapers. Consequently, while I was developing my "spiritual" side, I was, to a large extent, detached from many very important things. It was only after I became aware of the things I have already discussed that I realized I had to do a lot of "catching up" on a lot of issues.

As I have attempted to inform, educate—and sometimes, agitate—other Christians on the vital issues, I have been met headlong with the same mind-set I myself had for years. A college dean of mine used to say that "some Christians are so heavenly minded that they are no earthly good, and some are so earthly minded they are no heavenly good."

Many Christians, I have found, have developed a sort of schizophrenia about their relationship to God and this earth. I know it was true in my case. They have the ability to compartmentalize the various aspects of their lives. Mentally, they have one compartment that they label "spiritual." This contains such things as church, Bible reading, prayer, witnessing, giving, and personal development.

On the other hand they have a compartment that they call "secular." This one contains such things as career, job, education, politics, world affairs, the economy, the arts, entertainment, and much of our social contact with the rest of society. And they do a very good job of not mixing the two. They go to church to develop their spiritual lives and then look to "secular" sources for everything else.

But in fact there should be no distinction between secular and spiritual in the mind of the Christian. Everything is spiritual in nature: world affairs, government, economics, the arts, politics. For example, the worldwide movement of Marxism-Leninism is a "spiritual" movement. It is militant atheism, and atheism is as much a religion as is Christianity. Or, take the case of economics: if you believe that God owns all things, then you must agree that even the making and spending of money should be guided by Christian principles. So you are not being "unspiritual" when you get involved in all areas of life.

For years I was confused when I saw very sincere Christians who were active in church, sang in the choir, taught Sunday school, served on the deacon board, and shared their faith, who then went out on election day and voted for a candidate who stood for things that were blatantly anti-Christian and an insult to decent people. This in spite of the fact that the stands the candidates had taken on important moral issues had been widely circulated in the Christian community.

Such actions by the Christian community have troubled me, and I've tried to figure it out. I think I have discovered, at least in a small part, why it happens that way.

Most of us would agree that intelligent people can make intelligent decisions if they have the proper information. That's a fair statement, isn't it? We also know that we will make bad decisions if we have bad or incomplete information. As we say in the computer age, "Garbage in, garbage out."

So, what seems to be the answer? I believe part of the problem—a major part—within the Christian community is in the area of *information*.

While many churches are not to be faulted in developing what they call the "spiritual," they can be faulted in accepting and perpetuating the myth that Christians, in order to be "spiritual," should not concern themselves with such things as world affairs, politics, the school system, national defense, and the economy. In fact, many of us can attend church for years and never hear a discussion on public education, politics, or religious persecution in a foreign country.

Reading between the lines and hearing beyond the journalistic jargon in the reporting of world news is much more difficult than in national news. Whereas my friend in Chicago could listen to those pro-choice interviews and know the people were lying because she knew people who were involved in the pro-life cause, we cannot test world news against our personal experience. Few of us can go to Russia or China or East Berlin to see for ourselves what is happening. We must, unfortunately, rely on second-hand sources. In adult Sunday school classes and study groups, local churches can begin to discuss religious and political persecution in other countries. They can read and discuss books such as this one. Members who are associated with journalism or book publishing or magazines or newspapers can help fellow Christians become aware of the techniques which can be used to distort the news. (Many I have discussed in this book.)

I remember how the United States waited outside Berlin for the Russians, our supposed allies, to join us in the invasion of Germany's capital. A few years after that we watched as an ugly wall was erected to divide the city into two sectors—east and west. Then we watched as men, women, and children jumped from second-story windows to get over the wall and to freedom in West Berlin. Some crawled across in the darkness on their bellies. We watched as many of them were gunned down by Russian soldiers. We watched as people marked the graves of the fallen with flowers. Yet we did nothing.

When I think about the Russian invasion of Hungary, I can still hear the faint voice of a Hungarian freedom fighter coming over shortwave radio saying to America, "Help us, please. The Russians are killing our people. Please help us." But we did nothing. We appeased the aggressor and allowed him to snuff out the faint voice of freedom in Hungary. We heard the gunshots in the background and were told of the massacres as a brave people tried to withstand Communist domination. Yet we did nothing. America lapsed into silence. And we went about our everyday business as if nothing had happened.

Over the years several of these aging, brave Hungarian freedom fighters have called in to "Point of View" and told us they were there when the Russian tanks crushed their revolution. They still ask the question, "Why didn't you help us?" And I have no answer, except to say we're doing the same thing to the people of Cuba, Angola, and Nicaragua.

But contrast this ominous silence with the newscasts on September 10, 1989, which told of the president of Hungary telling thousands of refugees from East Berlin, "You are free to cross our borders into Austria," a bold statement which violated an agreement between the Communist bloc nations. Again the United States watched. But this time we heard shouts and applause. We saw tears. We felt joy. There are moments when one believes that the world is good after all. And there is a reason to hope. This was such a moment.

The next few days we watched our television screens in awe as thousands of refugees, most of them young and talented, walked and ran and drove across the Hungarian border into Austria—and freedom.

That same week evangelist Luis Palau conducted preaching missions in the Soviet Union, in such cities as Moscow, Riga, Kiev, and for the first time in a hundred years, in Leningrad. In conjunction, Bible Literature International (BLI) printed one million religious booklets on Russian presses inside the Soviet Union to be used during the religious meetings.

In fact, I talked "live" on "Point of View" with Jim

Falkenberg, president of BLI, on a special telephone hookup from Leningrad. He told us of the thousands who attended the meetings and of the deep hunger of the people to hear the biblical messages and receive the literature.

The meetings were historic in that this was the first time since the 1917 revolution that major Soviet churches—including the Russian Orthodox church and the All Union Council of Evangelistic Christian Baptists of the USSR, as well as many of the "unregistered" churches—worked together in an open evangelistic outreach.

On the downside, the historical pattern has been that after a period of friendliness and accommodation toward the church, the Communist regime has launched a new period of religious persecution. For example, during the 1920s Stalin tolerated the church until his economic recovery programs were complete. Then in 1960, as soon as he felt he no longer needed their cooperation, Nikita Khrushchev ended his accommodation of the church.

So, while we applaud the benefits of glasnost and perestroika and the new freedoms the people are enjoying, we're still looking over our shoulders at history.

Madison Avenue
Marxist

I wouldn't have thought it possible if I hadn't seen it unfolding on the television screen before me: Mikhail Gorbachev was strutting across the room, straightening his tie Johnny Carson style. His smile was broad and friendly; his demeanor, confident and sincere. As he approached Secretary of State George Shultz, who was himself smiling effusively, Gorbachev thrust out his right hand. And there, posed in front of a bright red flag bearing the hammer and sickle, the two shook hands like old buddies.

Said the announcer doing the voice-over: "Gorbachev, in fact, is doing so well, one question is: 'Why?' How can a man who brought so few answers on the question of human rights and whose troops are still in Afghanistan *get away with it?*"

How indeed? Every American man and woman watching the proceedings surrounding Gorbachev's trip to the United States should have echoed: "How *can* he get away with it?"

Because I myself am a broadcaster, I am constantly confronted with the media and the way in which the news is broadcast to the American people. I see the distortion, the bias, the behind-the-scenes editorializing. And the most frightening part of it is that the public is buying it all. What they see broadcast on the evening news or printed in the

183

newspaper or in the news magazine, most accept as truth.

Not long ago I was the guest on a talk show to discuss my book, *The Selling of Gorbachev*. A gentleman called in and said, "Well, you know, Mikhail Gorbachev has given up on socialism. He says it doesn't work." That man was wrong, tragically wrong, and I told him so. In no way does Mikhail Gorbachev intend to move away from socialism. What he does want to do is build a better, stronger Leninist socialism. He has never said otherwise.

A while back, Clark Bowers, director of the Claremont Institute's Commission on US-USSR Relations and an expert on understanding the Soviets, was my guest on "Point of View." Here is what Clark told me: "The issue isn't whether or not the Soviets are choosing Western-style Jeffersonian democracy or the Leninist style. Gorbachev has been very clear that the Leninist path is the one they've chosen and that they will never deviate from that path."

Those aren't my words. That's what the expert says. But that's not what we see paraded before us on our televisions and newspapers. As I watched the coverage of Gorbachev's visit and as I monitored the news feeds coming into the newsroom here at the USA Radio Network, an uneasy realization grew within me. Instead of the much-touted summit for world peace, I was watching a staged media event, an extravaganza, a monumental hype.

The official Washington community acted as if this were a state holiday. Red carpets greeted Gorbachev at the airports, and sirens screamed as his limousines whizzed through the streets of our nation's capitol. The Soviet flag flew over the White House as the honored guests enjoyed lavish state dinners and an official coziness, usually reserved for our trusted allies and close friends. With unrestrained enthusiasm, Washington welcomed the top man of the evil empire. America was gripped with "Gorbymania."

Gorbachev has been such a good story and has managed to romance journalists in such a way that he has managed to get terrific press.

Late one night, after watching a television program featuring clips of the smiling, dapper Communist, I lay back on my pillow, laced my fingers behind my head, stared into the blackness of the room, and marveled at the smoothness, the finesse, the sophistication of the entire campaign. It was a textbook case on how to switch the label on a package, yet leave the product inside unchanged. Now here it was, being sold to the American public as "new and improved." We were being subjected to the slickest, the most deadly, public relations campaign in the history of our country.

Just what is this campaign? Why, it's the packaging and merchandising of the Kremlin boss himself. It is an attempt to change the image of Communism so that it will no longer be repugnant to democratic Americans. And what an all-pervasive campaign it was! Whatever I watched on television, wherever I looked for reading material, I couldn't escape the party chief. He was interviewed on American television by Tom Brokaw on NBC; he appeared on the covers of the major magazines; he was showcased on all three major television networks. Americans were urged to believe Gorbachev was just as honest and sincere as the insurance salesman who lives next door with his pretty wife and two kids.

Mikhail Gorbachev isn't the first Soviet party chief to make his presence felt in our country. Remember the spectacle of the blustering, bullying Nikita Khrushchev banging his shoe on the table at the United Nations? It was he who lectured the world that Communism would eventually triumph. How well I remember that day in June of 1957 when Khrushchev appeared on nationwide television and told the American people, "I can prophesy that your grandchildren in America will live under socialism. And please do not be afraid of that. Your grandchildren . . . will not understand how their grandparents did not understand the progressive nature of a socialist society."

Here is the big question: Is Gorbachev really different from Khrushchev and other such Communists? Our American media says he is. They tell us he's a new kind of Communist, that he can be trusted because he's given up on the idea of ruling the world. It's a nice thought, isn't it? Too bad the facts don't bear it out.

The truth is that Gorbachev is determined to fulfill the prophecy of Khrushchev and every Communist warlord since Lenin. Whenever Gorbachev's status as a true believer in Communism has been tested, he has always passed with flying colors. Why do you suppose Gorbachev was selected for his present position of power? It was because his fellow followers of Marxism-Leninism firmly believed he was the person best qualified to advance world Communism.

What Americans don't understand is that Gorbachev has been especially groomed by the propaganda pundits of the Kremlin to be sold to the West. Evidently the majority of our news personnel don't understand this either.

"The problem is," Clark Bowers, the director of the Claremont Institute's Commission on U.S.-USSR Relations, told us, "the American media are by and large putting words into Gorbachev's mouth, words that he and the Communist party have never stated."

No, the Soviets have no intention of lifting the yoke of Communism. Nor do they plan to change their system. Glasnost, you see, is not for the Russian people. It's for export. It's for you and me. The entire public relations campaign is a ploy to lull the American people into complacency. All they have to do is get us to believe the evil empire has adopted the openness and freedom of Western democracies.

There is no question that we are seeing deep and dramatic changes in the world, especially in Eastern Europe. Can we every forget the emotions, shared by millions around the world, as we watched the faces of the East Berliners emerging from their dark city of despair into freedom's light in West Berlin? There was awe and wonder in their eyes when, for the first time, they saw and felt and touched freedom. Or who will ever forget the throng of people who stood defiantly atop the Berlin Wall? Or forget the sound of the hammers as they desperately chipped away at this ugly monument to man's inhumanity to man? Or can we ever explain our joy at seeing hundreds of thousands take to the streets in Budapest and Prague, raising their voices, chanting to their Communist oppressors that "not is the time to set the captives free"?

Although Gorbachev's glasnost has helped to unleash the pent-up hopes of millions, it is true that he has suddenly given up on Communism and their Grand Design for world domination. While he is crying to "reform the system," the masses are demanding pluralistic institutions, free elections, self-determination for all people, a chance to work in a free-market ecomony, and an end to the Communist Party's domination. They, in fact, want to see and end to Communism itself. It all springs from a grass-roots democracy movement, not out of the kindness of Comunist heart.

While millions cry "freedom," Gorbachev insists that his goal is the consolidation and perfection of socialism, not its destruction. He's been very open about it, if we would only listen.

During the upheavals in Europe, Gorbachev published a manifesto across two pages in *Pravda* on November 26, 1989, insisting that "Marxism will be revived in the Soviet Union, and under the leadership of the Communist Party." In a revealing statement he insisted, "Today we face the difficult challenge of reviving the authority of Marxist thought, the Marxist approach to reality. At this complex stage the party *must keep its monopoly on political power.*"[1]

The "manifesto" intentionally emphasized his program's "Marxist-Leninist roots." In it he stated that "Lenin might have been wrong about one central point in his philosophy—that there can be no intermediate phase between capitalism and socialism."[2]

Dr. Fred Swartz told the "Point of View" audience, "A Communist has total moral maneuverability. Nothing is right or wrong, only what advances Communism is right." So, for instance, Gorbachev can use religious freedom to eventually *destroy* religion, or embrace capitalistic ideas and methods in order to gain the power to destroy capitalism. The Communists will "take three steps forward and two steps back." But their goal is always *Communism.* They believe it will inevitably triumph.

What we're seeing in Gorbachev is a very adroit Marxist-Leninist *embracing* "an intermediate phase" between capitalism and socialism in order to strengthen Communism. He exposed himself, once again, as a hard-core, doctrinaire Marxist-Leninist when he said, "The new face of socialism is its human face; this fully corresponds to the thought of Marx. Because its creation is the chief goal of restructuring, we can with full justification say we are building human socialism."[3]

Except among a specific class of hardliners in the Communist world—and on some university campuses in America—Communism as an ideology, is *dead!* But the Soviet military is stronger than ever. The Soviet Union still has the mightiest millitary establishment in the world, and it's very much in place and geared for action. Many Soviet-watchers believe that they are playing a deadly game by exaggerating their current economic problems in order to pressure the gullible West into bailing them out once again before the Soviet military/industrial establishment suffers serious erosion.

I asked Clark Bowers about Communist honesty. Here's what he told me: "It's the way their words are covered, the way they're said with a smile. It's the half-truths. And as Dennison once said, 'The lie that is a half-truth is the blackest of lies.'"

Is the Kremlin's campaign of disinformation working on the American people? You bet it is! Recent surveys show just how effectively. For example, national polls conducted in 1983 and 1985 indicated that the majority of Americans viewed the USSR as a growing threat, but of those polled now, only 31 percent see Russia that way. Sixty-seven percent say the threat is exaggerated. In 1984, 56 percent believed the Soviet Union "is like Hitler's Germany—an evil empire trying to rule the world." But by 1987, 58 percent *denied* this assertion.

Remember the "Puff Gorbachev Campaign" just prior to his summit meeting with President Reagan in December 1987? It was so successful that our perception of the military threat from the Kremlin dropped alarmingly. Thanks to the pro-Soviet coverage in our own media, Communist boss Gorbachev enjoyed an amazing rating among American voters: 66 percent favorable, 22 percent unfavorable. A whopping 71 percent perceived him as "different" from previous Soviet leaders.

It was on December 4, 1987, just days before the Summit, that Peter Jennings announced on ABC evening news that President Reagan had an approval rating with the American people just slightly higher than that of Gorbachev. What irony! We viewed Mikhail Gorbachev, a Communist henchman, almost as favorably as the President of the United States!

There's more. In a poll conducted by the Gallup organization in December 1987, Gorbachev was named as one of the "10 Men Most Admired by Americans." He finished in an eighth-place tie with Lee Iacocca, the chairman of Chrysler Corporation. The Gallup spokesperson stated, ". . . political figures and personalities who receive extensive media exposure dominate the selections." With the right press, Adolf Hitler himself could have looked good!

Any good public relations person knows the secret: if you want to reach the American people, get your product or personality on television. It's best to choose a prestigious show, one with a trusted TV personality to act as host and interviewer. Pick someone who won't ask embarrassing questions, someone who will allow your client to dominate the interview. That way he will be able to get his views past the interviewer and into the homes of the American people.

Oh yes, one more thing—perhaps it's the most important of all. When your client is interviewed on television, be sure he is showcased as "being in charge," as a forceful, energetic person. And most of all, he absolutely *must* come across as a "nice guy."

Well, the Soviet imagemakers found a network and an interviewer who would give them what they wanted. The network was NBC, and the interviewer was the innocuous Tom Brokaw. True to form, Brokaw allowed Gorbachev to engage, virtually unchallenged, in an hour-long exhibition of cunning manipulation, blatant lying, evasion, and Kremlin-style browbeating.

Said Representative John Porter (R-IL) after viewing the program: "I had hoped to find a man of candor and some measure of sensitivity and integrity. What I heard and saw was a consummate propagandist, adroit at deception and perpetuating the lies that in the end will stifle any real hope for improved United States-Soviet relations."

Gorbachev certainly understands the media. On television, he stated he had received many thousands of letters from Americans. What he *didn't* say was that many Americans, including members of Congress, had sent thousands of letters protesting Soviet human rights violations—none of which, I might add, received a reply.

When asked about the rape of Afghanistan, Gorbachev replied, "They appealed to us. . . . Meeting their desires we introduced our limited Soviet contingent of troops."

That's not how Abul Shams, former economic advisor to the president of Afghanistan, tells it. He said the Soviets lied to his government, telling them that the United States was at that very moment poised on their border ready to invade. Once in, the Soviets murdered the government officials in cold blood. That very night they slaughtered seventeen thousand people on the streets of the capital city!

Here is the message Shams had for us, the American people: "We trusted the Soviets. We signed treaties. We signed agreements. Do not think the Soviets will honor treaties with you any more than they did with Afghanistan. Don't trust the Russians. We did, and we lost our country."

Evidently Tom Brokaw didn't think these facts were all that important, or surely he would have brought them up. Or maybe it was just that he didn't want to offend the Communist leader.

David Zurawik, television editor for the *Dallas Times-Herald*, wrote of the NBC Gorbachev event that it was an example of television as an "awesome mechanism of propaganda, capable of shaping public opinion almost overnight." He continued: "It only took [Gorbachev] one hour on prime-time TV in an interview he took away from questioner Tom Brokaw. The next day, an ABC News poll put Gorbachev popularity at a 59 percent favorable rating, only four points behind Reagan's. . . . Soviet Jewry? Afghanistan? Poland? The Berlin Wall? Forget it. We liked the way he came across in the intimacy of our living rooms. We'll vote for him."[4]

The media told us that a Marxist-Leninist, an international thug bent on conquering the world, is to be as trusted as a freely elected President of the United States. And you know what? Americans are believing it!

Isn't it time we wake up to the power the media wields over us? Most of us feel informed and entertained by it, never thinking of its potential to mold our concept of reality. But all the while it is shaping our images, our perceptions, our morals, our prejudices and biases about people, events, political movements, and world leaders. No conquering general or despotic ruler ever had the power to mold men's minds as do those who control our modern mass media. With such media control, the Antichrist could become as acceptable to us as Teddy Roosevelt! Sobering thought, isn't it?

While observing the savoir faire of Gorbachev and his handlers, I asked myself over and over, *How can he know us so well? Why is it he so perfectly understands the American mind and media?* Then, one day, on my way back from meetings in Washington, I came across a very interesting little book at a newsstand at Washington National Airport. In that book I discovered the key I had been looking for.

The title of the book was *Mikhail S. Gorbachev: An Intimate Biography.* It was written by the editors of *Time* magazine. (That's right. The same people who named him "Man of the Year.") On the cover was a picture of Mikhail and Raisa Gorbachev. On the back cover was printed this heartwarming little blurb: "With colorful writing and thorough research, *Time* tells the story of how a hero of Soviet labor wins the sweetheart of Moscow State U., rises through the ranks of the Communist Party and becomes the leader of America's most dangerous adversary—and one of the most remarkable leaders of our times."

Here's what I discovered in that little book: A man by the name of Alexander Yakovlev had quite a bit to do with educating Gorbachev (the entire Communist braintrust, in fact) in the ways the media can be used to manipulate the American public. Before teaming up with Gorbachev, Yakovlev himself had been steadily climbing his way up the political ladder in Moscow. Then, in a political struggle within the inner sanctum of the party bosses, he came out the loser. Stripped of his Central Committee job, he was sent to Canada to fill the post of Soviet ambassador, an assignment tantamount to stamping "The End" on a political career. But Yakovlev became an expert at his main function as Soviet ambassador to Canada—U.S. watching.

Yakovlev was, in fact, well suited for the job, having attended Columbia University in New York City during the late 1950s. His stay in Canada allowed him to spend endless hours monitoring American television, gaining an understanding of how the television industry persuades, manipulates, forms opinion, and sells everything from toothpaste to automobiles. He made special note of the kinds of people Americans respond to, whether they are preachers or politicians.

It was when Gorbachev, a member of the Supreme Soviet, visited Canada in 1983 that he and Yakovlev met for the first time. They hit it off well. Despite his familiarity with McDonald's hamburgers, beer commercials, and American TV, Yakovlev was still what he had always been— a bitter critic of the United States. Two years later, Gorbachev became general secretary of the Soviet Union. Guess who he appointed his chief of propaganda and trusted media advisor? You got it—Yakovlev.

Ironic, isn't it? Yakovlev, the bitter critic of the United States, is the man responsible for pumping out the public relations drivel that is flooding our country. No wonder the entire PR campaign shows a disdain for our system of government and reveals the arrogance of the propagandists who are manipulating the American people.

"Instead of putting words into his mouth, why don't people just read Mikhail Gorbachev for what he really says?" I asked Clark Bowers.

"Because they look to the sources of information we have in America today," Clark answered. "It's only normal and natural that they not see the man for what he is because that's not what they see on the nightly news nor what they read in the morning newspaper. How many people take the time to go and do research from primary sources or to read the long text of his speeches? So how can Americans ever *know* what he actually said?"

That's the American media as we have them today. Whatever those folks tell us, we believe. What else are we to do?

It's not surprising that the Soviet propagandists are working so hard to portray Gorbachev as a warm, caring leader who wants more "open" relations with the United States. What *is* incredible is the way our media are beating the drum for him, the way they are telling us he is a new type of Soviet leader, that we can trust him because he is a modern man who wants only peace and prosperity for his country and the world. Our own news sources are refusing to report to us, the American people, the truth about Mikhail Gorbachev and his true goals.

Yes, the major networks do massage and censor the news. They do make it fit their predetermined views about what we should know. And that withholding of information, that distorting of facts, is right now swaying the citizens of our free country toward actually embracing a Soviet dictator and his oppressive Communist views.

WHAT CAN WE DO?

Since we live and breathe in a society totally submerged in messages and sales pitches, biased news and information, entertainment with hidden messages, and outright propaganda—all of it beamed at us with space-age technology and unlimited funds—we must learn to cope with it and to inoculate ourselves and our families against its influence. If we can't handle it, we will surely be seduced by it.

Learning to cope is not an easy process. At times it's downright threatening. The problem is, we tend to be very comfortable with our longheld assumptions and behavior patterns.

When Thomas Schuman was our guest on "Point of View," he warned us repeatedly about the consequences of allowing the Communists to accomplish their seduction of our nation. Barry from west Texas called in and said, "There's a good part of the American public who want to remain ignorant in order to pursue a comfortable lifestyle rather than protect their freedom."

"That's true," Mr. Schuman replied. "But I wouldn't blame the average American because, let's face it, the average person in the United States is too busy. He has to wake up at six A.M. and take his kids to school and take his cars for repairs and buy cat food on the way back home and quarrel with his wife. It's the elitists I blame. They are the real traitors."

I wholeheartedly agree. Average Americans are just too busy to find out for themselves.

Many, many times I've emphasized how important it is that at least a solid core group of concerned citizens here in the United States understand the Communist mind and the forces and powers doing battle in our world today. The rest of the people are going to take their six packs in their pickup trucks and drive to the lake, or they're going to sit like couch potatoes and watch the sleaze on television.

The question is, To which group will you belong? If you are a concerned Christian determined to make a difference in our country, you have a responsibility not only to understand what is going on, but also to be able to communicate it. You should be able to talk knowledgeably to your neighbors and friends, to your teachers and classmates, to your minister and your church—to anyone and everyone with whom you come in contact.

For an hour and a half a day, five days a week, I talk with many of you on "Point of View." I'm going to be honest with you. One of my biggest frustrations is time. We just don't have enough of it! As far as educating people goes, all we can do is scratch the surface. We're simply not able to get out all the information that needs to be gotten out. That's why I encourage our listeners to read well-researched materials.

In many of the books we recommend, the information you need is all laid out for you in good form. You can discuss the subject with your family or your friends. Or, if you are a student, you can take this information and reason competently with your teacher on the subject of Communism.

When you see headlines and news stories, you'll be able to talk about them intelligently. And you will be able to give some sound reasons for your views.

You may not be able to vote in Congress or speak before the Senate, but you can become a part of that small core of informed experts on Communism and other political issues. Take the time and make the effort to become educated on a subject that may well determine the future of every one of us.

You can find books and magazines and listen to radio and television programs that will give you the other side of the news. You just have to dig deeply to find them.

PART FOUR

WINDOWS ON THE WORLD

News from Another Pers

Something had been bothering me for a couple of years. Although I knew the problem, I couldn't quite put it into words. The thing was, it seemed a bit inconsistent to me for a Christian radio station to spend fifty-five minutes preaching the gospel and sharing the truth with their listeners, then to pause for five minutes of "news" from a network or wire service that was liberal, left of center, and in many instances hostile to the conservative Christian worldview.

One day, while flying back from Colorado with my oldest son, Mark, I had an all-too-rare opportunity for a real talk with him. I decided to use him as a sounding board for my frustration. During our conversation, I told Mark some of the dreams I had for the future. He had just recently graduated from Texas A&M University and was working for a large firm in Dallas.

"What I'm going to share with you is just a dream," I said. "Right now it's no more than a vision. And it just might be that it will never get beyond that stage. But I believe in this dream, Mark. I believe so much that I'm determined to try it."

I went ahead to explain my conviction that the American people were not getting the truth from our national news media. I said that someone should develop an alternaive news source. "The thing is," I told Mark, "the opportunity to do just that might be lying right in front of us."

I went ahead to explain that we had already bought time on a satellite for "Point of View." "We pay all that money and we're only using the satellite space ninety minutes a day, just the length of the program," I told him.

"Why not just buy the time you actually need?" Mark asked.

"We can't. We have to purchase the satellite space full time—twenty-four hours per day—whether we need it or not. And that's what is challenging me. I don't want to see that other 22.5 hours go to waste every day."

Many nights I had lain awake, thinking about that satellite twenty-three thousand miles out in space and dreaming of ways to use it to reach America.

"Information—" I told Mark, "that's what the American people need. Truth without the liberal slant. My vision is to get into the news business."

I told Mark I was convinced there were radio stations all across America whose personnel felt exactly as I did—sick and tired of the major networks' monopoly over news and information.

"Surely they, too, must be looking for a viable, professional alternative. And now, through satellite technology, we can build a network of radio stations that will opt to carry our news broadcasts in lieu of those of the major networks. What we will do is broadcast five minutes of news at the top of each hour, put it up on satellite, then invite radio stations across America to carry it."

I had shared this vision with several people in the past. What I usually got back was a blank stare. No one seemed to have the slightest inkling of what I was trying to accomplish or how I would do it. I wasn't sure that Mark would understand, either.

"What do you think?" I asked.

For a while he said nothing. But after giving the idea

careful thought, he answered, "It's a good idea, Dad. It would be good for America."

That's all the encouragement I needed. Right then and there, in the skies between Colorado and Texas, I hired Mark as business administrator for the soon-to-be-formed company.

Things don't happen overnight; I learned that a long time ago. It took two years of research and hard work to bring my vision to reality. But in October, 1985, the USA Radio Network broadcast its first newscast on satellite.

While "Point of View" is produced by International Christian Media and is supported by contributions from its listeners, USA Radio Network, Inc., is a commercial enterprise. It's out in the work-a-day world slugging it out with the rest of the companies for a piece of the national advertising dollar. And we're being successful.

Sometimes we forget that this is America, and we operate in the free enterprise system. While many people will give a few dollars to a ministry, they don't feel comfortable investing heavy dollars in an enterprise such as quality radio and television broadcasting.

But investment opportunities are out there. And if we want to change the way people think and desire to develop alternative, quality radio and television programming, we need to put our money on the line. Sure, we may lose it if we don't invest wisely, but that's the chance we take when we invest in anything. That's free enterprise.

The Christian community has long been sadly lacking in the area of social information. Too many of us have no idea what is going on in the world around us. Churches, you see, can do an admirable job of teaching on "acceptable" subjects, yet fail to give their people any information on many other vital issues. Christians are left to learn from some other source, usually the national news media and the entertainment industry.

Some Christians are so disgusted with mainline newspapers and news shows that they refuse to read or watch anymore. All they do is engage in a general carping condemnation. Others understand the problems of the media in abstractions, but as consumers they tend to accept what they read and see as generally accurate. After all, the camera doesn't lie, does it?

Sadly, it does. And many people I talk to have given up on the media news, saying it's no longer important to them.

"At one point, the media were showing Christians as ignorant, backward people," said Jean, a caller from Illinois. "Now they've had programs on where they show the whole movement, as they call it, as *dangerous*. The editing, the background music, the photography—they try to make it look like the evangelical movement is some sinister plot to take over the United States."

I have to tell you, I agree with Jean. There was a point at which the national media was saying, "These people are a little ignorant; let's ignore them." But now there is a rising tide in the national media saying that these people are not only ignorant, but dangerous."

Within the last few years we have seen a revolution in radio. Some of the changes have been good, and some have been bad. One of the most phenomenal revolutions has been in the area of what I call "Christian information radio."

"Point of View," which is carried on over 25 percent of all Christian radio stations—as well as many general format stations—has had a part in awakening the conservative and Christian communities to the importance of giving out information on social and moral issues, politics, the media, religious freedom, and the rising tide of intolerance of the Christian faith in America. In fact, our program was presented with the National Religious Broadcasters Award of Merit at the 1986 NRB convention in Washington, D.C., for our "pioneering efforts in satellite programs on Christian radio."

I believe the success of "Point of View" and of Christian information radio generally has paved the way for USA Radio Network News. But, despite its overwhelming appeal to Christian radio, USA Radio Network News is not "Christian" news. In fact, a superficial listener wouldn't distinguish it from any other network newscast. And that's the way it will stay.

We have to be extremely careful in the way we write and broadcast the news. It's impossible, you see, to translate raw data through any human agency without its being interpreted by that individual's worldview.

News is like history. It's translated through what we already perceive to be truth. One news journalist may be predominantly a secular humanist while another holds to a Christian worldview. Both have access to the same facts. Even if both try to be as fair and honest as possible, the worldview of each will undeniably and inevitably affect the selection and interpretations of the news.

That may sound as if our news is simply the other side of the liberal news coin, but there is one major difference: we face these realities of bias and admit them up front. Many in the major networks, on the other hand, work overtime trying to convince you that their news is totally objective.

In this journalistic day and age, we can never have *unbiased* coverage. So what we need is *balanced* coverage. If we're going to be shown the liberal side, we had better be shown the conservative side as well.

While USA Radio Network News is in-depth, professional, hard news coverage, it is not a right-wing antidote to the liberal opposition. The difference, you see, is not in what we put in or take out. The difference is in the worldview with which we approach the facts.

It is important to listen to news you can trust. As I explain to our news staff, "Point of View" is a program of opinion, of various viewpoints—and it is billed as such. But it is our news staff's job to present a fair and objective, professionally delivered news report every hour, on the hour, twenty-four broadcasts a day, every single day of the year.

We train our news people to avoid what is called "rip and read"—that is, taking the wire services copy and simply reading it over the air. Even though we subscribe to the wire services, we usually have to do "major surgery" on the copy before we can present it over the air. Many of the stories, although billed as hard news, are so laden with liberal-leftist buzzwords, clichés, spins, and zingers that we are forced to train our writers to recognize the objectionable sections and excise them in their rewrites.

Just before Operation Rescue held a demonstration in Los Angeles, California, I found Paul Baker, one of our staff members, steaming over a piece that had just come in over the United Press International (UPI) wire service. Their lead sentence read, "With *militant* antiabortionists *threatening* three days of *disruptive protests,* police Wednesday ordered an *emergency command post* manned and doubled the deployment of officers in some areas" (emphasis added).

Talk about biased reporting! It sounded as if Rescuers were rifle-toting assault terrorists instead of nonviolent demonstrators.

Well, Paul couldn't stand it. He just had to do something.

"I called UPI and asked to be connected with James Ryan, the author of this article," Paul told me. "When Mr. Ryan came on the line I asked him, 'Can you tell me where the balance is in this story? It reads like an editorial or a commentary. Where is a discussion of Operation Rescue's own opinion of what's going on? And, furthermore, why are terms like "militancy," "threatening," and "disruptive" used when people are sitting in front of a door going limp when they're arrested and dragged away? Where does it say in this article that they're nonviolent?'

"Mr. Ryan answered, 'It says that.'

"'Where?' I said. 'I don't see it.'

"There was a click on the phone; then he came back a minute later and he said, 'Looks like they dropped that paragraph.'

"I asked who it was that snipped that part away, and Mr. Ryan's answer was, 'I don't believe that's any of your concern.'

"I said, 'Excuse me, but I believe we're paying you hundreds of dollars a week to receive your news service. That makes it our business! I'd like to know when there's going to be a rerun of that story to go through.'

"'Well, I don't think you're going to see a rerun,' Mr. Ryan said.

"I told him I certainly thought we should. Or we should at least see some sort of balanced story to counteract the story that just went over.

"About three and a half hours later, the story came over in its uncut version. And all of a sudden there was a balanced story. Oh, there were a lot of expressions against pro-lifers still there—that inflammatory first paragraph was still in—but it was a different story. Whereas the first lead had read, 'Police gird for antiabortion protest,' the new one said, 'Elected officials call group dangerous. Group says it's nonviolent, but expects violence from opponents.'"

This need for editing is not an occasional thing. It's a constant. There's a continuous flow of biased writing being sold as "objective" reporting. And as careful and well-intentioned as a person may be, without a trained eye he may easily find himself unwittingly mouthing somebody else's biased interpretation of the news.

That's why it is vital that we have men and women on our news staff who are first-rate professionals.

If you want to know a first-class newsman, you ought to meet John Clemens. John wears suspenders and an open collar, and toward the end of the day he begins to look a little frayed around the edges. But John is one good news-man. As they say, he lives, eats, sleeps, and breathes news. He's a news junkie. His idea of a day off is to come to the newsroom a half hour late and stay all day.

John Clemens is the news director of the USA Radio Network.

After accumulating over twenty years of experience in the news business, John "burned out." He had been a newsman for radio and television in New York, North Caro-lina, and Wisconsin. He had been a talk show host and a play-by-play announcer for baseball. In short, he had run the full gamut of broadcasting. But when it came to news, John was tired of exploiting people or—as he puts it—of "al-lowing myself to be a conduit for projecting the liberal view-point."

The event that finally made John Clemens decide to leave the news business came when the television station for which he worked assigned him to cover a bus accident. He described the scene as "trying to interview these little children with broken teeth and cut mouths and banged heads." And he tells of seeing parents "pushing these in-jured kids into answering my questions with this bright light and a video camera and microphone stuck in their faces.

"These children had just gone through a traumatic ex-perience. We're talking about little four- and five-year-old kids here! They've got their mouths sewed up with stitches, and now their parents are pushing them to 'An-swer his question, Sally!' And all because they wanted to get their kids on television.

"I mean, it's exploitation in its purest form. This was one of the last stories I did before I made up my mind to get out of broadcasting."

But I knew John Clemens was a good newsman. That's why I asked him to come to work for us.

As we sat and talked together, I described to John my vision of what the network could be. I told him we were determined to do something different with the news. We wanted to be honest and to report things in a forthright manner.

John later told me that when he found out about the opportunity to come to work for USA Radio Network and do straightforward, hard-hitting news without parroting the liberal line, he couldn't wait to get back in the business. He told me recently, "You know, at this job I look forward to coming to work every day! Even on days I don't have to be here, I come anyway because of the excitement."

And exciting it is!

One of the most impressive things about the network is that we've been able, under John Clemens's direction, to establish scores of correspondents around the world. At the latest count we had trained professional journalists, who file stories for USA Radio Network in over forty countries around the world.

A few days ago John told me, "Marlin, it's funny, but our foreign correspondents are more conservative in their general reporting about news that happens in their countries than the news we get from the major wire services. For these overseas correspondents, conservatism seems to come naturally. Here in the United States, journalists have heard so much liberal bias that they begin to mimic the reports and catchphrases that are constantly used."

Sometimes when I need my batteries charged, I'll stroll into the news room. It's like plugging into a two-twenty power source. I call it "controlled mayhem." Computers hum; four newswires spit out copy; a bank of telephone lines, four television sets, two radios, and short-wave radios monitor the BBC, Radio Moscow, Fidel Castro's Radio Havana, and other foreign sources. And they're all on—at the same time—24 hours a day, 365 days a year.

If you came into the newsroom at three o'clock in the morning and if we didn't have a clock on the wall to tell you what time it was, you wouldn't know whether it was three o'clock A.M. or nine o'clock P.M. For when it's three A.M. in Dallas, our people in the Philippines and in Australia, Tokyo, Seoul, and Hong Kong are filing their reports because over there it's daytime.

Conversely, at three o'clock in the afternoon it's just as busy, plus we have the closing stock market and commodities reports. We have wall clocks on the newsroom wall set to the current times in Moscow, London, Tokyo, and Dallas.

In the newsroom you can't help but be aware of the fact that news affects you—just as it affects me—and it's always happening somewhere. It's a big world out there with twenty-four different time zones, and we cover them all.

We rely a great deal on our people in foreign cities to tell us what's happening where they live. At home we rely heavily upon our affiliated radio stations to let us know what's going on in their communities.

One thing we determined early on was to develop our own sources for stories rather than sit at the wire service machine and wait for the stories to be written for us. We prefer to write our own, and we're good at it. When Delta flight 1141 crashed in Dallas on August 31, 1988, we had reporters on the scene within minutes. We were the ones who gave eyewitness accounts to our affiliate stations. One large wire service, in fact, depended on USA Radio Network reporters to furnish them with reports.

When John Clemens came to work at the network, I told him I felt we had hundreds of built-in newspeople who work at our affiliate stations, who could become the eyes and ears of the network. Then I asked him to develop these people to reach our goal of covering the nation.

A clear example of how effective we've been in developing this idea centers around what became a national story—a schoolyard shooting in Stockton, California. Before the major networks knew anything about it, we got the first word from radio station KCJH, our affiliate in Stockton.

Somebody living in the neighborhood heard the gunshots, went down the street, and saw what had happened. Immediately she went back into her home and called our affiliate, who promptly called us. We had the information on the air in minutes, interviewing the woman who saw it and talking to both emergency squad people and others who were there. We were able to do this because our affiliate radio station in Stockton alerted us to the situation so quickly, and then we were able to send it instantly around the nation via satellite.

I also told John I wanted to develop our own expert pool, sources for commentary and opinion on current news and events. I was tired of seeing the same dirty dozen dominate the television screens on all the national networks. Washington is filled with people who hold to a conservative viewpoint, but the major networks won't give them the time of day, much less six minutes on the David Brinkley show. I wanted to give these people a platform upon which they could express their opinions to the American people.

Now, don't misunderstand me. We do get commentary from the liberal side as well as from the conservative side. But it's giving conservatives a chance to comment that makes ours a balanced report. Giving both sides is what makes us different.

Has it worked? You bet it has! We have two giant files loaded with the names and telephone numbers of people who are experts on a variety of subjects. Take the Soviet Union, for example: we have a dozen experts, authors who work at different think tanks, congress members, senators, and Sovietologists, as well as dozens of other sources. So when something big happens in the Soviet Union, such as a change in the politburo, we know exactly where to go and the people to whom we should talk to get an intelligent evaluation and interpretation of the breaking story.

We are constantly listening to our competition, too. We know what ABC, NBC, CBS, and CNN are doing. We're always gathering information. There is more material coming into our newsroom than we are ever able to use. We put five minutes of news at the top of the hour around the clock, but there are times when thirty minutes each hour wouldn't be enough to cover the material we have available.

That's our hardest job: condensing the news and de-terminating what is the most important story for that par-ticular hour—that is, which story affects the largest number of listeners. We're constantly keeping our eye on our goal, our mission: to disseminate the news and infor-mation properly and to present it professionally so that the people in our listening audience will be able to make intelli-gent decisions about the world around them.

One night while I was watching a program on tele-vision, a particular commercial caught my attention. It was over so quickly that it didn't quite register. So I kept looking for it to be replayed. Sure enough, a few weeks later it came on, and I was able to get a closer look at it. What I saw absolutely dumbfounded me.

The commercial had a weird hue to it. It was almost occult in tone. Its meaning was profound, far beyond what the writers and producers hoped the general public would pick up, I'm sure.

Here's what I saw: The spot opened by showing sort of a combination machine/robot with flashing eyes and smoke blowing from it. It was awesome. Out in front were men dressed in expensive business suits and carrying brief-cases. They approached the machine/robot very slowly and with extreme care, a look of wonder and fear in their eyes.

Then, as one, all the businessmen knelt in front of the machine/robot. It was as if mere mortals were kneeling be-fore some electronic god. As they knelt, a voice said: "When information is in the hands of a few—you are at their mercy. You play by their rules!"

It was a commercial for AT&T. Yet it was more than just a commercial. It was almost prophetic.

Those who wrote and produced that commercial have enormous insight into the power of information. They know and understand that whoever controls information will control the world.

We in America must think ahead to the twenty-first century. When my engineer friend told me the technology was there for those who were visionary in their outlook, my thoughts centered on the consequences of someone's actually controlling it. The very future of civilization depends on who seizes this awesome opportunity.

Had Christians not abdicated their responsibilities within society, we wouldn't have to worry about the control and use of the media. Lies have been able to triumph because they have largely gone unchallenged. People who would normally bring in an opposing voice have been shut out by those who control the mass media in our country.

As we move ahead into the future, we must think seriously about who is going to control this crucial flow of information. Will it be the Kremlin? Will it be the United States government—or perhaps the large supranational corporations? Will it be the people who are now in control of the major networks and media outlets? Or will it be an awakened citizenry? Will the church have any input into how this information is used?

John Naisbitt wrote a best selling book entitled *Megatrends*. Although I disagree with Mr. Naisbitt's futuristic New Age conclusions, I have to admit he's right on with some of his statements. He wrote:

> 1957 marked the beginning of the Information Revolution. The Russians launched Sputnik, the missing technological catalyst in a growing information society. The real importance of Sputnik is not that it began the Space Age, but that it introduced the era of Global Satellite Communica-

tions. The space shuttle has a lot more to do with the Globalized Information Economy than it will ever have to do, in our lifetime, with space exploration.

In 1950 only 17 percent of us worked in information jobs. Now more than 65 percent of us work with information, as programmers, teachers, clerks, bank technicians. . . .[1]

Scientific information is currently growing about 13 percent per year. If information systems increase as anticipated, some predict that by the year 2000, the annual rate could jump above 30 percent. And by the year 2000, the blue-collar workers will make up only 10 percent of the American work force.

This new technology has ushered us into a new phase and intensity in the battle for people's minds. And make no mistake, those who control this unprecedented power will wield it over our minds and our children's minds as well. The media have established one of the most significant spiritual battlegrounds ever witnessed by humanity.

Whoever controls this new technology has instant access to the minds of millions. As of this moment, it is virtually controlled by people hostile to our Christian faith. And those people are using their control to launch an all-out attack upon it.

America needs alternative broadcasting. Unfortunately, Christian television hasn't fulfilled its great promise of being a viable alternative to secular broadcasting. While there were moments when Christian TV came close to measuring up to its potential, for the most part it has been made up of entertaining fluff and mental pabulum.

An enormous opportunity was handed the Christian community, but it was squandered on the promotion of personalities, dubious crusades, and fundraising techniques so questionable they remind us of that consummate religious shyster, Elmer Gantry. No gimmick, it seems, is too "far out" to try.

The biggest scam of all is the continuous promise that if you send in a large donation, you will receive in exchange instant health, wealth, and happiness. This is nothing but an appeal to the old "something for nothing" mentality. It shamelessly victimizes people who are already struggling desperately to keep their heads above water spiritually, mentally, and financially.

Since much of Christian radio and television are supported by freewill gifts from the listening or viewing audience, it is legitimate to spend a certain portion of the broadcast in fund-raising. But if the broadcaster has to spend an inordinate amount of time appealing for money, then God may be trying to tell him something—perhaps that he needs to find another line of work.

With few exceptions, Christian television and radio do not deal with the hard issues facing us all. Even though young people are being bombarded with secular humanism, premarital sex, homosexuality, evolution, AIDS, pornography, occultism, rock music, filthy movies, and all kinds of pressure from their peer groups, Christian radio and television seldom seem to deal with these things. Their programming just is not geared to giving answers to the questions people are asking.

America still needs alternative broadcasting. Many had hoped Ted Turner's venture into the news business would present our nation with a viable alternative to the present system. But, while his Cable News Network does a credible job in some instances, many of us are concerned about the direction Mr. Turner seems to be taking his new-found power as a communications mogul.

What Ted Turner seems to be saying is that he sees nothing wrong with the Soviet dictatorship; he is making movies of the Soviet Union that could just as well be travelogues produced by Novosti Press. Many of us are concerned about the way he chooses to overlook the diabolical nature of the Communist system. And as he promotes his "better world society," many of us are asking just what kind of society it would be. In an article in *Fortune* magazine (July 7, 1986) Mr. Turner stated, "Communism is fine with me. It's part of the fabric of life on this planet." To the contrary, some of us see Communism as part of the fabric of death.

One event that gave us a bit of insight into Mr. Turner's belief system and his growing power was his *CNN World Report* Contributors Conference in Atlanta in May 1989. Mr. Turner hosted such luminaries as Bob Geldof, former President Jimmy Carter, Afghanistan's Prince Sadruddin Aga Khan, Costa Rican President Oscar Arias, Coretta Scott King, Georgia Governor Joe Frank Harris, Atlanta Mayor Andrew Young, and 180 television journalists from 90 countries.

While I was reading a report of this conference in the *Dallas Morning News,* I came across some things I found very revealing—and very disturbing—about Mr. Turner. The article stated that Mr. Turner said he "owes his latter-day global perspective to Fidel Castro, whom he visited in Cuba seven years ago." Although Mr. Turner was "prepared to encounter a Cuba of 'tanks on every corner, machine guns and unhappy people,' he instead found himself disarmed by Mr. Castro, who taped an endorsement of CNN during the visit."

Mr. Turner has long positioned himself as a moralist out to slay the "big three" commercial networks, which he says are run by people with no social conscience. When he first came on the scene, many of us breathed a silent prayer that here, perhaps, we finally had a man who would use his vast communications empire to restore some decency in America. After hearing his ramblings for several years, however, many now believe he is only going to add to our problems.

Take, for example, his remarks at the close of the conference, as reported by the *Dallas Morning News*. In what was characterized as a "rambling speech on brotherhood," Mr. Turner told the audience, "Your delegates to the

United Nations are not as important as the people in this room. We are the ones that determine what the people's attitudes are. It's in our hands."[2]

He then called the Christian religion a "religion for losers." Here's how the *Dallas Morning News* reported his remarks: "Christ died on the cross, but he needn't have bothered, Mr. Turner says, 'I don't want anybody to die for me. I've had a few drinks and a few girlfriends and if that's gonna put me in hell, well, then so be it. . . .'"[3]

Then, reflecting his one-world ambitions and New Age thought, he appealed to his listeners: "'Why don't we broadcasters make it our goal to get the world at peace by the year 2000?' he asked. 'Let's make it the year zero—BP and AP. Before Peace and After Peace.'"[4]

Yet another verbal attack on people who disagree with Mr. Turner's "enlightened" world view prompted one of my semifamous "Soapbox" commentaries. Before the invention of radio, television, and public address systems, the oldtime politicians used to stand on platforms, tree stumps, boxes, or anything that would allow them to be seen and heard by an audience. So, radio being the "theater of the mind," I stand on my imaginary soapbox when I want to get something off my chest. I employ a few things from oldtime radio to make it interesting and entertaining. When I'm through with the commentary, I'll say, "Pardon me a moment while I get down off this soapbox and put it back into the closet." I'll then lean away from the microphone to make it sound as though I'm walking across the room. "Ah, here's the closet," I'll say as the engineer furnishes the sound of a door opening and closing. I then "walk" back to the microphone, straighten my tie, and continue with the program. It must be believable because when I go anywhere to speak, someone always asks me if I brought along my soapbox.

What prompted this particular soapbox commentary was Mr. Turner's prattling before a meeting of the National Cable Forum in Century City, California, where he referred to pro-life people as "bozos and idiots" while touting the pro-choice stance of an upcoming program on abortion on his TBS superstation (*Los Angeles Times*, "Newsmaker" column, July 14, 1989.) I sure wasn't going to let Mr. Turner's remarks go unchallenged!

Here's part of what I said from my soapbox: "Hey, did you see the little propaganda piece that Ted Turner ran on his television superstation? It was called 'Abortion for Survival' and was produced by Eleanor Smeal's organization—something called 'Fund for the Feminist Majority'. . . . Mr. Turner, who said, 'A child is not a child until it's born because you don't have funerals for miscarriages'[5] had stated that he hadn't even tried to sell commercials for the show, stating, 'We'll just take a lick for a night. You know, so it'll cost us 400 or 500 thousand dollars.'

"I sort of thought he was 'putting his money where his mouth was' until I saw the truth. The program turned out to be nothing more than a fund-raiser for Mr. Turner's Better World Society, complete with 800-number phone lines for memberships—at twenty-five dollars a pop, no less.

"Christina Pickles, former *St. Elsewhere* star, narrated the show and was advocating 'keeping abortion a legal and safe and simple procedure as a necessity for preserving women's lives.' For the life of me, when she was making her pitch for people to send in their money, she sounded just like one of the TV evangelists they criticize.

"Mr. Turner even attempted to con the viewing audience by staging a so-called 'objective' panel discussion after the program. In staging the 'debate,' he said, 'We'll give the other bozos a chance to talk back. They look like idiots anyway.' The pro-choice side of the panel was made up of Eleanor Smeal, whose organization produced the piece, and Faye Wattleton, the ever-present mouthpiece for Planned Parenthood. On the other side was Nellie Gray, head of March for Life, and Congressman Robert Dornan, who stated up front that the panel was stacked but that he came hoping he might get a few licks in for the pro-life side. My admiration for Dornan went up when he walked into that one-sided discussion. I think he's a master at cutting through the pro-abortion, Planned Parenthood piffle and getting right down to the facts of the matter. And the frustration on the faces of those on the other side testified to that fact.

"This little dog and pony show was narrated by Martin Agronsky, whose voice always takes me back to when I was a kid, leaning back against our big cabinet-style Zenith radio, tuned to radio station KFDM in Beaumont, Texas, listening to him and other news correspondents talk about war in faraway places. Unfortunately, it was not one of Mr. Agronsky's finest performances. Wish I hadn't seen him. Kinda shattered some of my hero myths about newscasters.

"Mr. Turner said that he owned the station and he has the right to editorialize. I agree with him on that. But I think Americans have the intelligence to recognize a one-sided, stacked, propaganda piece when they see one.

"In the final analysis it all seemed staged to prove Mr. Turner's assertions that all pro-lifers are 'bozos and idiots.' But it didn't work. We aren't that stupid yet."

I concluded by saying, "That's my 'soapbox' commentary for today. Now, excuse me while I put my soapbox back into the closet." (Sound man furnishes sound of door opening and closing, just like in old-time radio).

OPPORTUNITIES AND OPPOSITION

By now you may be saying to yourself that the situation is hopeless. On a few occasions over the years, I've felt the same way, and I have received many letters from listeners like Sam, who wrote me from Boston, Massachusetts.

"Marlin, I'm a businessman, a father of two nice teenage kids, and I sometimes despair over the kind of world we're going to leave them." His letter went on, "It seems that maybe we've already lost the battle for values and decency and should just give up."

I wrote him back and told him, "Hang in there, we're not licked yet!"

Sam is not alone. From the thousands of letters I receive, it's obvious that a lot of people feel overwhelmed and helpless when faced with these mounting problems. They begin to believe that there is nothing they or anybody can do.

That's why so many of them express their gratitude to me and my staff for meeting the issues head on. They are encouraged because they see us venture out to challenge the big boys of the big media. And the fact that we are speaking up has encouraged thousands of them to speak up as well.

We, on the "Point of View" radio broadcast, want to continue to "make a difference." Our objective is to *impact* our nation.

We want to see changes in the spiritual life of America, first of all. That's priority one!

We want to see changes in public policy.

We want to see a return to traditional family values.

We want to see the end of the abortion industry and the killing of unborn children.

We want to see the end of the attacks on Christians from the media, movies, and television.

We want to see changes in the public schools, starting with the textbooks themselves.

We want to expose those forces bent on bringing about an anti-Christian, secular America.

We want to expose those who are promoting religious persecution and inhibiting free speech under the guise of "separation of church and state."

This is part of our game plan at "Point of View" radio.

We never lose sight of our goals. And we are daily advancing toward them.

I'm challenged by what lies ahead of us. I honestly believe that we are standing before the greatest door of opportunity ever presented to a generation of people—an opportunity to impact the nation and the world.

Unfortunately, many people, especially Christians, do not realize that opportunities always bring opposition and conflict. But conflict is part of this battle for the hearts and minds of people. While some people quit at the first sign of opposition, others are roused to action by it. Difficulties awaken their courage, stimulate their minds, and make them ready for the battle ahead.

Doors of opportunity do not stay open long. Many men have lost fortunes by not taking advantage of opportunities. An opportunity is like a priceless gem on the auction block—you only have a moment to bid before its gone.

Since I first started addressing the issues on radio almost two decades ago, I marvel at how active and involved the evangelical Christian people of America have become. It has taken years and years of hard work by a lot of people to educate and motivate, but these people have now become concerned—and involved—in the things that shape our lives. And America is feeling their force.

We are setting the agenda for national discussion on many vital issues. The liberal media would prefer *not* to discuss such things as *abortion, bias in the media,* and *religious persecution.* But they're being forced to because of the involvement of a cross-cultural, loosely-knit, religious and politically conservative coalition that numbers into the millions.

A few weeks before his inauguration, I was among a small group of evangelical leaders who met in the White House with President-elect George Bush. The meeting made me realize just how active the evangelical community has become.

I looked around that room and saw men and women who stood for the same things you and I stand for. And, like me, they were bringing the hopes, dreams, and ambitions of their friends to this man who was going to lead our nation.

During the meeting, each one of us around the table—Jerry Falwell, Dr. James Dobson, James Robison, Beverly LaHaye, and others—echoed a joint concern that we, as evangelicals, be included in the decision-making process of our country.

We expressed our concern that for too long, evangelical Christians have been a group to be sold a policy by the politicians *after* the decisions have already been made. And that if an administration wants the support of the pro-family, pro-life, evangelical Christian community, they must become more sensitive to our issues and invite us to participate in the decision-making, policy-setting process from the very beginning.

We're not naive. We know that in any administration—democrat or republican—we have enemies who will not only fight against our agenda, but will attempt to keep anyone who shares our values from holding a single position of influence or power anywhere in the government. So we're going to win some and we're going to lose some. But we should never again be content to sit at the back of the political bus.

Fortunately, there is a growing army of informed, active, conservatives and Christian people who understand that pushing for our agenda means confrontation, conflict, and opposition. But they also know that "opposition means opportunity."

We have been placed in a unique place in history. And I don't want to look back a few years from now and have to say we missed this opportunity to impact our nation.

After years of hard work we're now on the cutting edge in utilizing the latest, most sophisticated broadcast technology available. And we've only begun to realize the opportunities.

Through our use of satellite delivery systems, microwaves, computers, fiber optics, and other sophisticated equipment at "Point of View" radio, when something happens that needs to be communicated to the nation immediately, we're able to go on the air with an "action alert" and mobilize concerned citizens all across America *within minutes!*

But, as fascinating as that may be, the key to reaching this nation with our message is not technology or hardware or software or satellites in space.

The real key is *you!*

To everyone who asks if *one* person really can make a difference in this world, I answer a loud, resounding "Yes!"

Elections have been decided by *just one vote*.

Prayer was taken out of the public schools by Madelyn Murray O'Hair, *just one woman*.

Abortion on demand became the law of the land by *one woman,* Norma McCorvey, the "Roe" in Roe vs. Wade.

Movements have been started as the result of *one person's* vision.

Yes, one person can make a decided difference. *You* can make a difference. And you and I together, and the next person and the next person and the next . . .

You can take action by writing your congressman, joining a protest march against abortion, or calling the President's Opinion Line in Washington or your local radio and TV stations, or writing a letter, or gathering friends together to inform them about what's really going on.

Our goal is to bring about spiritual renewal by seeing America return to those basic, biblical fundamentals that have made it the envy of the world—a city set on a hill.

These are enormous challenges that will mean work, sacrifice, and the giving of our time, talents, and resources.

Winston Churchill's words to the people of Great Britain, as the dark clouds of World War II were gathering throughout Europe, should serve as a sober reminder to us all:

> Still, if you will not fight for the right when you can easily win without bloodshed; if you will not fight when your victory will be sure and not too costly; you may come to the moment when you will have to fight with all the odds against you and only a precarious chance of survival. There may even be a worse case. You may have to fight when there is no hope of victory, because it is better to perish than live as slaves.[6]

How we respond to the challenges before us could determine the *survival of America as a free nation!*

NOTES

Chapter 3   What Ever Happened to the Fun in the Funnies?

1. Ben Stein, *The View from Sunset Boulevard* (New York: Doubleday, 1980), pp. 83–84.
2. James Hitchcock,
3. Don Wildmon, *The Last Temptation of Jesus,* 7 July 1988. Tape #1458, USA Radio Network, Dallas.
4. Laura Longley Babb, ed., *Of the Press, for the Press, and Others, Too* (Boston: Houghton Mifflin, 1976), pp. 34–35.
5. Charles Wiley, *True Journalism,* 19 May 1987. Tape No. 1230, USA Radio Network, Dallas.
6. Babb, *Of the Press,* p. 30.
7. Donna Woolfolk Cross, *Mediaspeak* (New York: Putnam, 1983), p. 60.

Chapter 4   The Millionaire Evening Stars

1. S. Robert Lichter, Stanley Rothman, and Linda S. Richter, *The Media Elite: America's New Power Brokers* (Bethesda, MD: Adler and Adler, 1986), p. 22.
2. Jann S. Wenner, as quoted by A. Frank Reel in *The Networks: How They Stole the Show* (New York: Charles Scribner's Sons, 1979), p. 100.
3. Ibid., "Introduction."
4. Reed Irvine, *Media World View,* 26 Jan. 1987. Tape No. 1163, USA Radio Network, Dallas.
5. Ibid.
6. Helen Caldicott, *Missile Envy: The Arms Race and Nuclear War* (New York: Bantam Books), p. 311–312.
7. Brent Bozell, *Media Bias in Campaign Coverage,* 29 Aug. 1988. Tape No. 1485, USA Radio Network, Dallas.
8. Ibid.
9. Ibid.
10. "Trust in the Press, but Not the Enquirer," *Psychology Today,* May 1989, p. 13.

Chapter 5   Don't Blame the Press, Blame the Dominant Culture

1. Irvine, *AIM Report,* "Media World View," Washington, D.C., December 1987, p. 3.
2. Lichter, Rothman, and Richter, *The Media Elite,* p. 22.
3. Dinesh D'Souza, "TV News: The Politics of Social Climbing," *Human Events,* 16 Aug. 1986, p. 12.
4. Ibid., p. 13.
5. Ibid., p. 12.
6. Ibid.
7. Ibid.
8. Ibid.

Chapter 6   Fairy Tales About Abortion

1. *New York Times,* 6 Aug. 1989.
2. *New York Post,* 27 Sept. 1989.
3. Bill Carter, "Questions of Method and Morality in the CBS News Case," *New York Times,* 4 Oct. 1989 (emphasis added).
4. Tom Shales, "Playing Games with the News," *Washington Post,* 28 July 1989.
5. Richard Zoglin, "Star Power," *Time,* 7 Aug. 1989.

6. Ibid.
7. *Los Angeles Times*, 23 Sept. 1989, pt. 4, pp. 1, 9.
8. Ibid.
9. Ibid.

Chapter 7 Fairy Tales About Woodstock, AIDS, and School Textbooks

1. Wayne Slates, *Dallas Morning News*, 21 Feb. 1969.
1. *Newsweek*, 25 Aug. 1969, p. 88.
2. *New York Times*, 18 Aug. 1969, p. 25.
3. Ibid.
4. Ibid.
5. Barry Farrell, "Woodstock," *Life*, 5 Sept. 1969, p. 12.
6. Ibid.
7. Cal Thomas, "Cal Thomas Column," *Dallas Morning News*, 17 July 1987.
8. George Will, "George Will Column," *Dallas Morning News*, 6 June 1987.
9. Kerby Anderson, "Fundamentalist Christians," *Dallas Morning News*, 3 Nov. 1986.
10. David Aikman *The Summit Journal*, September 1988, p. 4.
11. Judy Weidman, Stewart Hoover, "A Study in Religion and Reporting," *Religious News Service*, 5 October 1987.

Chapter 8 Retelling the News from Nicaragua

1. Reed Irvine, Media World View, 26 Jan. 1967. Tape No. 1162, USA Radio Network, Dallas.
2. Larry Speaks, *Speaking Out* (New York: Avon Books, 1988), pp. 367–368.
3. Robert Curran, *Spiro Agnew: Spokesman for America*

Chapter 9 War of Words

1. George Orwell, *1984* (New York: Harcourt, Brace and Jovanovich, 1949), p. 175–178.

Chapter 10 We Rescue the Evil Empire—Again

1. A. M. Rosenthal, Rosenthal column, *Dallas Times Herald*, 4 January 1988.

Chapter 11 Madison Avenue Marxist

1. "Gorbachev Reaffirms Marxism," *Dallas Morning News*, 27 November 1989, p. 1, emphasis added.
2. Ibid.
3. Ibid.
4. David Zurawik, *Dallas Times Herald*, 4 Dec. 1987.

Chapter 12 News from Another Perspective

1. John Naisbitt, *Megatrends* (New York: Warner Books, 1982), pp. 2, 4, 5.
2. Ed Bark, Bark column, *Dallas Morning News*, 16 May 1989.
3. Ibid.
4. Ibid.
5. Ibid.
6. Ibid.
7. Winston Churchill, quoted in *Freedom's Fight* newsletter, Washington, D.C. August 1984, p. 3.